Become the Person You're Meant to Be

*Realizing Your Full Potential
As A Child of God*

Books by
Bryce Duane Bartruff

Insight: Uncommon Sense for Common People

A Pocket Guide To The Sayings of Jesus

Personal Prayer and Bible Study Notebook

Here Am I, Send Me: The Recruitement, Management and Training of Volunteers

Become the Person You're Meant to Be

*Realizing Your Full Potential
As A Child of God*

Bryce Duane Bartruff, PhD

Christian Focus Publications

Soli Deo Gloria

For Kevin and Kerri,
that they may glorify God
in all they do.

© 1993 Bryce Duane Bartruff
ISBN 1 85792 064 3

Published by
Christian Focus Publications Ltd
Geanies House, Fearn, Ross-shire,
IV20 1TW, Scotland, Great Britain.

Printed and bound in Great Britain
by Cox & Wyman Ltd, Reading, Berkshire

Cover design
by
Donna Macleod

CONTENTS

ACKNOWLEDGEMENTS

Special thanks to the many missionaries of the *American Missionary Fellowship* whose advice and insights helped with the formation and refinement of this material. This includes Kathy, my wife and friend who has worked hard to help our family live according to the principles in this material; and my parents Rev. and Mrs. Bryce O. Bartruff whose insights and personal lives were instrumental in laying the foundation for this book.

Thanks also goes to Dr. Stuart Sacks, Dr. Eugene Williams, Rev. Claire Harstad and Mrs. Jean Andreozzi who spent many hours reading through this material and making valuable suggestions for change; and Rev. Jim Gerhart and Mr. David Pennington for their support and comradeship. Finally that they might be encouraged for their labors, appreciation is extended to the many students who have worked through this material as a self-study course of the educational program of the *American Missionary Fellowship*.

INTRODUCTION

> **What kind of people does God use?**
> **Ordinary people - with all the struggles, all the strengths,**
> **and all the weaknesses of people like us.**
> **Its not what you are that's important;**
> **the issue is what you are willing to become.**
> **John MacArthur, Jr.**

A multi-volume encyclopedia could easily be compiled on the subject of personal growth and development. Including all aspects of this topic would be an impossible task; therefore the most critical aspects have been selected for this book.

The thrust of this material is to guide Christian men and women toward a better understanding of themselves and others. It is designed to help direct them toward becoming the type of people which they feel God wants them to be. This study is not intended to provide a complete listing of the answers for a full and powerful life. It is, however, designed to serve as a guideline for Christians who wish to take positive steps toward understanding themselves, their potential, and how this potential can be developed to glorify God most effectively.

This book was developed to provide systematic exploration of the fundamental characteristics which make up a person's inner being. It is designed to help Christian men and women learn how, under God's guidance, to control the direction of their lives and their life work.

Many of the assignments are probing and may tend to make the reader uneasy. This is natural. Self-honesty while difficult is important to the effectiveness of this material, as are discipline and hard work. Any marked growth of lasting quality requires a healthy dose of reality along with tenacity and self-discipline.

This concept was summarized by a successful Christian businessman who commented on the reference others made toward his 'luck' in business. He stated, 'It seems the harder I work, the luckier I get.' Obviously, the harder he worked, the more he gained. In the same manner the Christian reader will receive from this study only what he or she puts into it.

In developing this book every effort has been made to make it both interesting and challenging as well as insightful and thought-provoking. The words 'realistic' and 'holistic' reflect the general tenor of this material.

Realistic

Most believers have been taught that they should not dwell excessively upon themselves, and rightly so. People who are overly concerned about themselves may become selfish or proud. As a result they will have little time for others. But emotionally healthy Christians need to have a realistic view of who they are and what resources God has given to them to be used for His glory. The word *realistic* is key. In order to know the opportunities God has for us we need to recognize the abilities and talents he has provided. More than one Christian has reduced his or her effectiveness because of failure to gain a realistic understanding of one's self.

One minister, for example, loved children and felt the need to share the stories of the scriptures with them. Not overly talented in story-telling or working with children, he found it difficult to hold their attention. A realistic view of himself revealed these deficiencies. Burdened with the need to teach children, he carefully examined his talents and skills. It was not long before he remembered a boyhood hobby of ventriloquism. He acquired a puppet, and after brushing up on his neglected skill, he developed an effective ministry teaching the message of the scriptures through ventriloquism. A realistic perspective of his strengths and weaknesses lead to a viable solution to his problem.

Holistic

A second word which describes the thrust of this material is *holistic*. In this sense *holistic* refers to the inclusion of every aspect of a person's life. Just as the many parts of a tree need to be wholesome before there can be healthy growth, so there are many aspects of a person's life which need to be sound. In order for us, as children of God, to grow and develop in a healthy manner, we need to pay attention to our physical, social, intellectual and psychological, as well as our spiritual, development. Each part relies upon the whole.

It is not uncommon for career oriented individuals to concentrate their efforts on their work and neglect other parts of their lives such as their family, spiritual life or physical health. One such person, fully intent upon excelling professionally, neglected to watch his weight. He was too busy for exercise or recreation. Time off was held to a minimum and socializing outside of his work was non-existent. Each waking minute was spent in some way related to his work. After several years of tireless effort he showed physical signs of continued stress. Burned out, he had to step away from his career. His body had run down and he developed a severe heart condition. He now needed time to rest and recuperate. Had he led a holistic and balanced life he could have maintained a steady pace and accomplished much more with his career.

In the pages that follow you will be asked to examine each area of your life. Careful consideration will be given to whether or not you are giving the correct amount of attention to each aspect so that you can achieve to your optimum potential.

The acorn is very small, but in the right environment it can grow to become a mighty oak. If one of the vital ingredients for growth is distorted, it will die. Too much or too little light, water, nutrients, heat and air (wind) will affect the growth of the tree. In the same manner prayer life, family life, friends, study, personal witnessing and professional developments all play an important part in helping a person to learn the careful balance which will provide a healthy ministry for Christ. Three ingredients which are central to healthy maturation are *time*, *action*, and *attitude*.

Time

According to Psychologist John Powell, most people realize only about ten percent of their life potential. This observation deserves careful contemplation. As children in God's royal household we have a responsibility to God. We are to develop the life which He has given to us so that He will be glorified. Growth cannot be rushed. It is an orderly and natural process.

Healthy, mature growth takes time. Psychologist Douglas J. Bol tells a story which aptly illustrates this point. A well-adjusted child loved and respected her parents. She wanted to grow up to be 'just like mommy'. On one occasion her parents noticed that she had become somewhat depressed. Asked what was distressing her, she finally shared her problem. She observed that her mother's body was mature and developed. The child, wanting to be 'just like mommy', was depressed because she had not yet developed. Try as she might, there was nothing she could do to accelerate her physical maturity. Development of any kind takes time. This applies to physical, mental, social, spiritual and any other areas. The natural process that time plays requires people to be patient and work toward their continued development on a gradual, systematic basis. The Lord does not expect a Christian to gain spiritual maturity immediately after conversion (I Corinthians 3:2). Different things are expected at different times. We are each responsible for consistent daily growth, but we are not each expected to be at the same level of maturity.

It was a wise man who wrote, 'I am not what I should be and I am not what I am going to be but I am not what I was.' As Christians we can't be all-knowing concerning every aspect of life. We can, however, continually strive 'toward the mark for the prize of the high calling of God' (Philippians 3:14 - KJV). Consistent and systematic growth is essential if we are to become all that God intends.

Action

The comedian Tom Smothers said that 'life is what happens while you're making other plans'. For many Christians this is an accurate description. Although most people have good intentions, only those who actually put their plans into action reap the rewards.

Noting his need to control his use of time better, one of my colleagues once stated, 'I'd love to take a course on time

management, but I just don't have the time.' This friend
failed to see the need to free himself from the things which
kept him from living and serving as the kind of person he
knew he should be. He did not take the action which would
have improved his life.

Each day God supplies his children with 86,400 seconds
of time. The Christian who effectively uses his time for Jesus
Christ has not left his ministry, family and future to chance.
A successful life comes from a succession of days filled with
directed activities. Each day there should be a renewed
commitment to give of oneself to Christ and to take whatever
action is necessary to fulfill that commitment.

Ezra Pound said, 'A slave is one who waits for someone
else to come and free him.' We are not slaves if we take the
initiative to ensure our personal daily growth. The man or
woman who does not take daily action to ensure becoming
the person God would have him or her become is letting life
'happen' while 'making other plans'.

Attitude

The effectiveness of this book, as with any learning medium,
is based largely upon the reader's receptiveness to it. A
person's values, beliefs, prejudices and personal history
influence his or her attitude. A willingness to accept new
ideas and an openness to the leading of God are essential.
When these ingredients are present, the principles presented
here can be understood more readily and adapted to the
individual's life.

In the following pages you will be introduced to principles
which will assist you to grow. A systematic process of daily
refinement will lead you to a better understanding of yourself,
the direction God would have you to grow, and specific steps

to lead you there.

Hard work is essential, but the outgrowth will be a more mature life with Christ. This life includes the bountiful blessings which are ours through Christ. A Christian leader should not neglect to take full advantage of the attributes given him. Miss Spiegelberg expressed it well in the following poem:

Lord,
I crawled
Across the barrenness
To you
With my empty cup
Uncertain
But asking
For any small drop
Of refreshment.
If only I had known you better
I'd have come
Running with a bucket.

(*Decision*, November 1974)

BIBLICAL OVERVIEW

I.

BIBLICAL OVERVIEW

Praise be to the God and Father of our Lord Jesus Christ,
who has blessed us in the heavenly realms
with every spiritual blessing in Christ . . .
In him we were also chosen,
having been predestined according to
the plan of him who works out everything in conformity
with the purpose of his will
in order that we, who were the first to hope in Christ,
might be for the praise of his glory.

Ephesians 1:3,11,12

Blessed with every spiritual blessing (Ephesians 1:3), Christians have been chosen to represent God and to bring honor and glory to Him (Ephesians 1:11,12).

The scriptures point to the very fascinating role that God has assigned to man. Although he was born in sin, man has the unique opportunity to glorify God. Even through the simple act of coming into fellowship with God, God is given honor (Ephesians 1:4-7). I Corinthians 10:31 (NIV) states, 'So whether you eat or drink or whatever you do, do it all for the glory of God.' Again in Matthew 5:16 (NIV) Jesus states, '... let your light shine before men, that they may see your good deeds and praise your Father in heaven.' An overriding theme throughout the scriptures is that through thought, action and being, man should strive to bring honor to his Lord.

Even before the creation of the earth, God chose some to be His adopted children. Psalm 139:13-17 reveals the concern and care that God took with the makeup of each person. Each hair, the color of the eyes, beauty marks, basic intelligence, talents and even malformations (Exodus 4:11) were determined for the ultimate glory of God. Verses 17 and 18 of Psalm 139 reveal the love and care which went into God's design for man.

> *How precious it is, Lord, to*
> *realize that you are thinking*
> *about me constantly! I can't*
> *even count how many times*
> *a day your thoughts turn*
> *toward me. And when I*
> *waken in the morning,*
> *you are still thinking of me! (Living Bible)*

God's love is far greater than man has the capacity to comprehend. With this kind of love, God determined the make-up of each person.

As Christians our responsibility is to accept the gifts which God has given us. Physical characteristics, mental capacities, talents and environmental background have each been supplied to bring glory to God.

During a large conference of ministers a speaker expressed his recognition that he was not a very handsome man. To emphasize the point that he accepted this aspect of his life he then leaned close to the microphone and whispered, 'I don't know about you, but I don't have the courage to tell God He goofed!' As children of God (I John

3:1), we need to accept the fact that God has chosen us and designed us to glorify Him. Each aspect of our lives was determined by God. What we do with our lives influences the degree to which we reflect His intent for us.

Christians should not be afraid to recognize the characteristics with which God has endowed them. The scriptures which speak to the importance of healthy humility also indicate that you should 'think of yourself with sober judgment, in accordance with the measure of faith God has given you' (Romans 12:3 - NIV). A realistic and accurate self-image is essential if these talents are to be developed and used for His glory.

Matthew 25:14-30 presents an excellent illustration of the significance of an accurate self-image. Christ tells the story of three servants. Each was entrusted with a different amount of money. They were to invest this money for their master during his extended absence. Upon his return two of the servants had doubled their investment. One had buried his money in the ground. The two who showed a profit were rewarded. The other was punished. Two had recognized exactly what it was that had been entrusted to them. They struck out to develop it to a greater potential. The other man indicated that he was overwhelmed by his responsibility and failed to improve the resource entrusted to him.

As Christians we have been given resources which are designed to bring glory to our Lord. If we fail to recognize them 'with sober judgment' we will not be able to develop them, thus overlooking the opportunity to bring glory to God. The Christian who continually dwells upon his shortcomings, refusing to recognize and develop the valuable qualities God has given to him, will deprive the Lord of what he is responsible for producing.

The pastor of a small country church provides a good example of what can be done when a person has an accurate perspective of his talents and gifts. This friend acknowledged that he did not have enough musical talent to even participate in congregational singing and he also did not excel in public speaking. He did, however, have deep insight into the understanding of people. He excelled in encouraging and guiding his congregation spiritually as individuals. Identifying his strengths and weaknesses, he delegated as much of the music to others as possible. He aggressively sought to develop his speaking skills and concentrated on building men and women through personalized discipleship and counseling. Within just a few years the group outgrew their worship facilities. New property was purchased and a building program began. This country pastor used sober judgment to discover the strong and weak areas of his life. He was then able to develop them so that he could best meet the needs of others.

It is important that we do not forget that we were designed 'for the praise of His (God's) glory' (Ephesians 1:6,11,12). Ephesians 1 describes believers as 'children of God'. Verse 5 describes them as 'adopted' members of God's family. As adopted children we have the promise of both the rights and the responsibilities which are part of belonging to a royal family. Far beyond the privileges that man could ever be worthy of, God has given to man the privilege of fellowship with Him through Christ and a responsible position on earth.

This position of nobility can be compared with a monarch in medieval times. During that period royal heirs had both privileges and responsibilities. They benefited from prestige and recognition. A majestic home, fine clothes and the best food were theirs. With these benefits, however, came certain obligations. This included the protection of their subjects from outside invaders, the collection of taxes, the economic development and growth of the kingdom, and the people's general welfare. The degree to which these responsibilities were carried out varied from king to king, but each member of the family had obligations which accompanied the benefits of royalty.

As children of God we also have duties. These obligations vary from individual to individual depending upon the qualities and opportunities given (Matthew 25). The personal preparation necessary to carry out these responsibilities is a continual process. The Apostle Paul describes the development of his personal characteristics as if he were running a race (I Corinthians 9:24-27 - KJV):

> *'Know ye not that they which*
> *run in a race run all, but one*
> *receiveth the prize? So run,*
> *that ye may obtain. And every*
> *man that striveth for the mastery*
> *is temperate in all things. Now*
> *they do it to obtain a corruptible*
> *crown; but we an incorruptible.*
> *I therefore so run, not as uncertainly;*
> *so fight I, not as one that beateth*
> *the air; but I keep under my body*
> *and bring it into subjection: lest that*
> *by any means, when I have preached*
> *to others, I myself should be a castaway.'*

In striving toward the goal Paul is not satisfied with second place. He continually worked and developed his skills and abilities. As children of God we too must continue to develop in every way possible so that the Lord will be glorified through our lives. A fable is told which further illustrates the importance of tenacity and hard work in personal development.

In ancient times a king called his wise men before him and asked for a compilation of all the wisdom of the ages. When the wise men returned to their king they presented him with seventeen thick columns of material. These they said contained the wisdom of the ages. The king's reaction was that he had neither the inclination nor the time to read through the material. He commanded that it be condensed. Reducing the material to a single volume, it was also rejected. Finally, the wise men confronted their leader with a single sentence. It was this sentence which he accepted as a compilation of the wisdom of the ages. The sentence simply read, 'There ain't no free lunch.'

If, as members of God's royal family, Christian men and women are to develop their abilities and effectively carry out their responsibilities, they must diligently and continually work at enhancing their talents. Developing the potential God has given to you is not easy, but with a tenacious self-discipline comes development of character and greater opportunities to glorify God.

Joseph, Job and David are examples of men who had developed depth of character. If they had not been diligent in developing their spiritual and personal skills, their roles in Biblical history could have been much different.

The strong oak tree does not develop its healthy, stout trunk or deep roots without struggle and effort. Each tiny root must push itself through the soil. Only then can each drop of moisture be absorbed and passed to other portions of the tree. Long, hard winters and hot, dry summers each add to the strength and character which ultimately make a tall, majestic tree able to withstand the most destructive of the natural elements.

The responsibility of God's children to do good works for Him should of course, not be confused with trying to earn God's favor. As a child of God our position ensures His approval and love. Any action we take is to demonstrate our love for Him and not to gain more of His love. Our Father's love for us is already complete and unconditional. It is not based upon our actions and we cannot add to it by anything we do. Our Father simply loves us because we are His children.

For this reason we should be delighted to do all that we can to glorify our Father with that which He has so freely given to us.

PERSONAL INTROSPECTION

II.

RECOGNIZING OUR PERSONAL RESPONSIBILITY

> Be very careful, then, how you live -
> not as unwise but as wise,
> making the most of every opportunity,
> because the days are evil (NIV).
> Ephesians 5: 15,16

Not long ago I had a discussion with a friend about *Humanism*. Part of our discussion concerned our understanding of what is at the core of this movement. We asked what is it that humanists are saying and why is it considered so wrong by the Christian community. One of the central issues that we discussed has to do with a person's destiny. That is, who is in charge of what will happen to a person in the future?

Humanists will say that man is in control. You can do whatever you want to do. All that you need is to dream a dream, set some goals and you can make it happen. It is difficult to convince an oncology patient or someone with renal failure of this. They know what they don't want and that they would do anything they could to have their cancer go into total remission or for their kidneys to function effectively again. In many ways man is not in total control of his destiny.

To illustrate further, let's consider the implications of the familiar statement, 'I don't want to win the battle only to loose the war.' This is also referred to as a Pyrrhic victory. A Pyrrhic victory is a term defining a victory so dearly won that it is almost a defeat. It is derived from a statement made by Pyrrhus, King of Epirus, who was one of the greatest generals of Hellenistic times. In 279 B.C. he defeated the Romans in Asculum (Southern Italy). In doing so the Roman army cut off and destroyed his supplies, leaving his army in very bad shape. When he was congratulated by his friends on his defeat of the Romans he exclaimed: 'Another such victory over the Romans and we are undone.'

Pyrrhus was a fierce man who did all that he could to take charge of his life and glean from life whatever he wanted. When for example in 303 B.C. he lost his throne to Neoptolemus he turned to Demetruis I Poliocertes to learn the art of war. Then with the aid of King Ptolemy I Soter he regained his throne in 297 B.C. where he ruled jointly with Neoptolemus. Later in 286 B.C. he turned on his former friend and mentor Demetrius I Poliocertes, the ruling king of Macedonia, by conquering half of Macedonia. Pyrrhus would not let anything hold him back. He believed he was in charge of his destiny and took whatever steps he found necessary to achieve his objective.

How did this great warrior, who loved to battle and capture what was not his, die? A likely answer would be that he fell during a great battle. Another logical conclusion would be that as an old and respected man, he died in his sleep, at the end of a long and powerful reign. Ironically, this is not what happened. In 272 B.C. a peasant woman, while standing on the roof of her house, threw a roof tile at him. It hit him on the head. He fell to the street and died.

Pyrrhus is listed among the great generals of his day but it was a roof tile thrown by a peasant woman that did him in.

He was able to conquer nations and command thousands of men but even this great general was not in full control of his destiny.

As believers, we can learn from history. Regardless of the steps that we take to insure our future, our fate lies in the hands of God. If we are to live or die, to prosper or suffer from poverty, have good or poor health, be talented or limited, have opportunities or be restricted, each depends upon the blessing of God and the intent that He has for us. We are here to worship Him with our lives and in doing so we need to play out our part the best that we can with that which He has given us.

Conversely we are not to fall into the grasp of fatalism. We do have control over much of our lives. This includes the attitude that we take toward our situation, be it good or difficult, and the effort that we take in reaching personal objectives.

The scriptures tell us in Ephesians 5:15, 16 that we are to make the most of every opportunity. This is our assignment. It necessitates our willingness to do our very best, invest the necessary time, remain tenaciously at our tasks, look at the possibilities of what can be accomplished and as servants of God to remain attune to our understanding of what God's will is for us. We must be dreamers and doers tenaciously investing of our time.

Dreamer and Doer

Charles Swindoll in his book *The Grace Awakening* tells the story of President Thomas Jefferson. Jefferson was traveling on horseback with some companions. They came to a river that had been swollen due to a recent downpour. The bridge had been washed away and so each rider had to ford the river against very swift currents. A stranger asked the President if he would ferry him across to the other side. Jefferson agreed. After reaching the other side a member of the party asked the stranger why, of all the people in the group, he had asked the President to take him across the river. The answer is one worth contemplation. 'All I know,' he said, 'is that on some of your faces was written the answer "No, I might not make it" and on some of them was the answer "Yes, I will make it." His was a "yes" face.'

There are lots of 'Idea Men' out there, people who can dream up great things for other people to do or who have ideas of how things should be done differently. What we need are more dreamers who have the courage and fortitude to be doers as well. Most anyone can dream but it takes courage to put that dream into action.

As men and women involved with the ministry it is our responsibility to be individuals who have the attitude of expectancy. We should look for possibilities to serve, establish plans and set about to bring these plans into reality. Of course being a trailblazer takes courage and courage is better caught then taught. The Apostle Paul had a 'yes' face. He was both a dreamer and a doer. He recognized the limitations which were imposed on him and dealt with them the best that he could. We can look to Paul as a model of someone from whom we can catch the image of courageousness and see possibilities within the most difficult of circumstances. As a 'doer' with a 'yes' face we can have the valor to do what is required to bring what we need to accomplish into reality.

Tenacity and Time

Peter Tchaikovsky was a man who maintained the course regardless of the circumstances. Even during the most discouraging situations, which at times caused him to become greatly depressed, he continued to go on with his mission of composition. Because of this tenacious development of his talent he was, in 1866, invited by Nicholas Rubinstein to teach composition and history at the new Moscow Conservatory. He loved composition and while in this position he continued to compose. Many of his pieces were of a style inconsistent with the norm of his day. In 1874 he created the Piano Concerto No. 1, in B Flat Minor. This was a piece with a grand flair that was very unusual for his day. When Nicholas Rubinstein, whom he admired greatly, first heard this piece he harshly criticized the piece calling it unplayable, clumsy and vulgar. Peter, a sensitive man, was very discouraged by this disapproval. He continued, however, to fine tune the piece and later introduced it to Hans von Burlow, one of the great conductors of the 19th century. Hans von Burlow fell in love with the piece and introduced it to the world by playing it in a concert in Boston in 1875. Its success was sensational. It caught on so well it has been a part of the repertoire of every great pianist since.

In spite of the harsh criticism of his much respected mentor, Peter Tchaikovsky knew what it was he wished to accomplish and stayed the course. Had he wavered as a result of his discouragements and personal feelings and not given of the time and effort needed to create more works we might never have heard such great pieces as Romeo and Juliet, Swan Lake, the Nutcracker and the favorites of many, March Slave, and his overture, 1812.

We too need to be committed to the challenges which lie

before us. With prayerful commitment we need to insure that the direction in which we are headed with our life and ministry is that which the Lord would have in mind for us. Firmly committed to His divine direction we should then stay the course, regardless of the circumstances. This can only be accomplished with a daily and firm commitment to the Lord, staying attune to his desires for us. This includes time alone with God each day. It also involves spiritual accountability with someone who will hear our desires and commitments and help us to maintain an even keel when we otherwise might veer away.

Humanism does not provide a proper approach for life, nor does fatalism. What we should desire is freedom in Christ. We have been placed in our life situations with the responsibility of remaining faithful to Him and making 'the best of every opportunity'. We are to be His instruments and to worship Him through our lives. It is important that we remember that in the drama of life it is today's performance that counts. Not past successes or failures. The question we should ask ourselves is, 'Who am I now and what am I doing today?'

RECOGNIZING THE NEED

'Self-knowledge is that acquaintance which shows us what we are, and what we ought to be, in order to our living comfortably and usefully here, and happily hereafter.'

John Mason

As Christian men and women we are children of God. Created by God, unique qualities distinguish each person one from the other. Physical characteristics, personal background, mental abilities and personalities provide a mosaic of countless possibilities for the pattern of our overall make-up. People are constantly changing. With these changes come a number of added variables in our distinctive make-up. It is no wonder that a person frequently asks, 'Who am I?' and struggles at the task of making some sense out of his or her existence.

The question, 'Who am I?' is very basic to man. The answer to this question forms the foundation of the process on which personal development is built. Without a clear understanding of what his or her talents are, a person will not be able to determine which direction to place the emphasis of refinement.

A realistic understanding of 'Who I am' gives the Christian a focal point upon which to turn. Attention can then be directed toward becoming more Christ-like both inwardly and in relationship to others. The man or woman without a firm grasp of who he or she is resembles a drowning person. The victim is so concerned about saving himself that he cannot reach out to help and save others. The man or woman who has not yet discovered who he or she is will find it difficult to grow either in character or in relationship to others.

This chapter is designed to direct you toward a brief yet healthful exploration of who you are. This personal assessment should provide a realistic base in which you can better capture the potential God intended for you.

REALIZING THE CHALLENGE

> 'No one who has not a complete knowledge of himself
> will ever have a true understanding of another.'
>
> Novalis

Inscribed in gold on the Greek temple at Delphos were Socrates' words, 'Know Thyself'. The 18th century English clergyman Caleb Bolton cites, 'He that knows himself, knows others; and he that is ignorant of himself could not write a very profound lecture on other men's heads.'

Down through the centuries, two questions which have plagued man are, 'How am I to understand myself?' and 'How am I to understand other people?' Just as a person needs to have a foundation upon which to build a program for personal growth and development, he needs to know what to expect from himself before he can concentrate on other people's actions and circumstances. The Christian must learn about himself, who he is, and what his needs are in order to effectively reach out to the needs of others. The old adage that a drowning man is too busy saving himself to help another aptly applies.

Knowledge about oneself can be threatening to some individuals and may require a great deal of effort. But it is necessary if a Christian is to pull himself out of the water and help to rescue others. Several ingredients essential to self-awareness include openness, honesty, interiority and change.

Openness
In order for a person to understand himself, he must be willing to explore his innermost being. It is not uncommon for a

person to decide that he would rather not know more about himself. This often stems from a fear of what may be found. Many people are not 'ready' to learn who they really are.

For the person who is ready, an exciting revelation of both personal qualities and limitations will be his. The Apostle Paul stated, 'In everything give thanks: for this is the will of God in Christ Jesus concerning you' (I Thessalonians 5:18 - KJV). Each talent, gift and set of circumstances should help a person gain a greater appreciation for the individuality which the Lord has given to him.

This is well illustrated by a bashful layman who approached his pastor asking if he could assist with Vacation Bible School. The pastor agreed. Undertaking studies at a nearby Bible College, he continued to contribute time to the church. As he ministered he sought to learn more about himself. He wrestled with his abilities and limitations, looking inside himself to learn more about the qualities God had given to him and how they could be of service. Shy by nature, he realized that if he wanted to be an effective minister of God, he must overcome his fear. Gradually he increased his exposure to people, first as a children's worker and later as a teacher and leader. As he progressed, he accepted the responsibility for a small adult Sunday School class. Added exposure to people led to greater responsibilities and ultimately speaking engagements. At the end of his tenure at the Bible College he was approached by a mission organization and asked to serve as a missionary. Because he was willing to be open to both his good and bad characteristics, he was able to enhance weaker areas. The result was an invitation to begin a career which would otherwise not have been available to him.

Honesty

Total and open honesty plays a vital role in self-awareness. One young lady at a youth camp enjoyed singing very much. Her family had encouraged her in her singing at home and she wanted to perform for others. In her zeal she asked if she could provide special music during the chapel services at camp. The program director recognizing her lack of talent tried to redirect her energies in other areas. Her continued insistence finally led him to explain that singing was not an area in which she excelled. Hurt but persistent she entered the talent hour. It was there, in front of her peers that she learned a very hurtful lesson. Her lack of talent resulted in a performance that was not well received. If she had a realistic understanding of her musical abilities she would not have had to experience the deep embarrassment of rejection and ridicule.

In the same manner each person should take an honest look at himself. People who have an honest and realistic awareness of who they are can avoid the pitfalls of misdirected talents and will be less likely to blame others for their circumstances. They will be better able to choose the direction in which they need to concentrate their energies.

Interiority

Dr. John Powell, theologian and psychologist, uses the term 'interiority' to describe the person who has 'explored himself.' Each individual is made up of many parts. Senses, emotions, past experiences, future expectations, family life, spiritual health, social background, medical history, psychological stability, and mental qualities all contribute to the make-up of the total person. The Christian needs to be aware of the numerous qualities which influence his make-up and give him the uniqueness which distinguishes who he is from others.

Like a diamond, each facets of a person can be viewed from different angles. Each observation will provide new insights. Of course we can't see all the facets of a diamond at one time, nor can we see or experience or know all aspects of self-hood at one time. Years of careful observation from more than one vantage point are necessary for a comprehensive understanding of oneself. A total understanding may not be possible, but a working understanding of how the many parts fit together is. Each person should strive toward this end.

Change

Man is constantly changing. As he encounters new life experiences he gains insights and knowledge. With added knowledge the world takes on new dimensions. As a result man encounters new life experiences and so the cycle begins again. All of life is under constant change. In order for a person to maintain an understanding of who he is, he must either place himself in an environment protected from rapid change or remain alert to the effects which his personal growth has upon his understanding of himself.

Everyone has at least some control over his own thoughts and actions. For each, the degree of this influence will vary depending upon circumstances. Customs, habits and social influence bring with them pressure to conform to the actions or thoughts of others. As a person learns to observe these influences, he will gain an increased awareness of how to free himself from their bonds. He can then choose the thoughts and actions which he believes will help him to best function as a dedicated child of God.

RUNNING THE RISK

You made all the delicate, inner parts of my body, and knit them together in my mother's womb. Thank you for making me so wonderfully complex! It is amazing to think about. Your workmanship is marvelous - and how well I know it. You were there while I was being formed in utter seclusion! You saw me before I was born and scheduled each day of my life before I began to breathe. Every day was recorded in your Book! How precious it is, Lord, to realize that you are thinking about me constantly! I can't even count how many times a day your thoughts turn toward me. And when I waken in the morning, you are still thinking of me!
Psalm 139:13-18 (Living Bible)

Psalm 139:13-18 reveals the love that our Lord has for each of His children. With special care He determined how we should look, what qualities we should possess and even the type of environment into which we would be born. The faithful Christian desires to be everything that the Lord intends for him to be and makes use of the qualities given to him.

Aside from God's unconditional loving acceptance, man lives in a world which often fails to accept him as God designed. Children seem to possess an almost inherent instinct to make fun of other children, especially if they appear to be different. Anyone who is peculiar from a child's point of view is apt to be verbally badgered. Instinctively, the victim of such abuse takes steps to protect himself. By remaining distant or intimidating others himself, he learns to play a role which will protect him from emotional injury.

The child also learns from his parents what roles and behaviors are acceptable. As he learns to control himself in a way which is acceptable to society, he may become fearful of revealing his true self to others. Over a period of years, this can lead to a fear of doing many of the things he would like to do if he were not inhibited. In many senses this is good. In others it is not. To be too inhibited to run through a sanctuary during a worship service is healthy. To be fearful of speaking during a discussion group may not be. Each person learns to play many roles in the drama of life. The part of a child, student, friend, parent and mate are each distinguishable roles which are played by almost everyone. A son or daughter is expected to act a certain way around his or her parents. This same person may, however, play the part of parent to his or her own children. Such roles help to provide an orderly structure for society.

Due to the very nature of society and the need for different roles, people must adjust their behavior to some degree as they play their parts. When a role or series of roles form a mask behind which someone hides, losing an understanding of his identity, he needs to step back and take an objective look at himself to see who he really is.

Such a view may be threatening. The real person behind the mask could be someone other than what that person desires to be. The practical joker may be a lonely and friendless man. The pious deaconess may be a frightened child. The authoritarian pastor may be an insecure little boy. It has been stated that, 'to reveal myself openly and honestly takes the rawest kind of courage'. The Romans had a sign in their shops that read, 'Caveat Emptor', meaning 'let the buyer beware, since he buys at his own risk'. In the same way, the person who dares to take a peek at his true self and explore who he truly is may find more than what he bargained for. It is for this reason that this material will present many of the insights needed to reveal the 'inner person' through a gradual, gentle process.

Some pain is to be expected. It is like coming out of a dark cave and feeling a painful sensation in your eyes at the first rays of the sun. After a while we become accustomed to the light, and the temporary pain is replaced with the permanent joy of seeing.

As one middle aged business manager stated after completing a comprehensive self evaluation, 'I am gaining a better understanding of myself and, you know, I kinda like this guy called me.'

The Christian who truly desires to become all that the Lord intends must gain an understanding of the potential and characteristics which comprise his make-up. Such an understanding necessitates that he become vulnerable to the risk of losing treasured ideals about himself. Without this understanding, it is difficult to concentrate on developing into an increasingly effective instrument of God.

REMAINING REALISTIC

'For by the grace given me I say to every one of you: Do not think of yourself more highly than you ought, but rather think of yourself with sober judgment, in accordance with the measure of faith God has given you.'

Romans 12:3 (NIV)

The intent of Romans 12:3 is to convey that the Christian should strive to acquire accurate insight into the ingredients which comprise his character. Though it warns us against thinking of ourselves more highly than we ought to think it also warns us against thinking of ourselves less highly than we ought to think. Thinking 'with sober judgment' means accepting ourselves as God made us, and not trying to be someone other than who we are. Such acceptance requires that we recognize the abilities we have are given to us by God.

This passage says nothing to advocate that a Christian should either run himself down or egotistically build himself up. Both are based upon a false premise. What is expressed is the desire that each person gain a clear view of himself. Only a picture which is taken in focus will result in a clear print. The person who does not view himself in proper perspective will gain a distorted image. Such things as false pride, pious humility or rationalization can fog an otherwise accurate self-image.

No one is entirely free from preconceived ideas about himself or rationalization. They form a buffer to protect a person from personal disappointment and the criticism of others. Protecting themselves from accepting the criticisms of others and the related loss of self-respect, people often cry the infamous words, 'yes, but'. This gives them an excuse for their actions. The brother who strikes his sister has a ready excuse for his actions: 'Yes, but she hit me first.' The unemployed sluggard cites rationalization for his dilemma: 'Yes, but I can't find a job in which I know I will be happy.' The glutton excuses his weight: 'Yes, but I don't feel well when I diet.' In each instance the person has an excuse or 'rationalization' for his actions.

The term 'rationalization' was first introduced in 1907 by

Ernest Jones. He used it to identify 'the technique of inventing acceptable interpretations of behavior which an impartial analysis would not substantiate ... the colored glasses through which we look at reality.'

This defense mechanism is an important part of any person's make-up and can be both healthful and destructive. While it can serve as a helpful buffer to cushion unkind accusations against one's character, it can also serve as means to shift the responsibilities for one's actions onto someone or something else.

In I Corinthians 7:18-24, Paul explains to his readers that they should accept themselves as they are.

Was a man already circumcised when he was called? He should not become uncircumcised. Was a man uncircumcised when he was called? He should not be circumcised. Circumcision is nothing and uncircumcision is nothing. Keeping God's commands is what counts. Each one should remain in the situation which he was in when God called him. Were you a slave when you were called? Don't let it trouble you - although if you can gain your freedom, do so. For he who was a slave when he was called by the Lord is the Lord's freed man; similarly, he who was a free man when he was called is Christ's slave. You were bought at a price; do not become slaves of men. Brothers, each man, as responsible to God, should remain in the situation God called him to. (NIV)

As children of God we are each responsible to gain a balanced view of whom we are. By coming to grips with our present situation, we can more clearly comprehend how to take advantage of the opportunities to serve God which lie before us. In the following pages we will cover some of the ingredients primary to this realization.

REFLECTION, RE-EVALUATION AND RE-INTERPRETATION

> 'Like physical food,
> it is not what we take in that affects us,
> but what we digest and assimilate.'
> LeRoy Elms

The Psalms are an outgrowth of the love relationship which existed between King David and God. In Psalm 119:97 David writes, 'O how I love thy law! it is my meditation all the day' (KJV). As he reflected upon the things of the Lord, their relationship grew. As he thought about his Lord, read, prayed and sang praises, the Psalms emerged. Today a special relationship is perceived in the form of the Psalms. They depict a growing intimacy between a man and his God. In times of struggle and triumph, heartache and joy, King David shared his thoughts and feelings in song. It was when he left his time of meditation that he fell prey to the arms of Bathsheba.

King David needed a great deal of time to think and pray during his early years. His identity changed. Once an obscure shepherd boy in the peace and solitude of the mountains, he became a national hero with all the pressures which accompany notoriety. In conflict with King Saul, he sought wisdom and strength. If David had forgone meditation upon the Lord, history might have proceeded differently.

As present day Christians meet the challenges of everyday

life, they need time to consider its complexities. Prayerful thought concerning difficult tasks may produce the wisdom necessary to tactfully guide the situations through to a healthful end. In the life of every believer there should be quiet time in every life for such reflection, re-evaluation and re-interpretation.

One pastor applied at the planning commission office for papers to build a new church. He learned from the authorities that there was community opposition to the church's acquisition of the property, spearheaded by a woman seemingly friendly with the church. According to the pastor's testimony, his first feelings were ones of dismay and hostility. As a result of prayerful reflection, re-evaluation and re-interpretation, he realized that the Lord understood the needs of the church. As the pastor, his duty was to restrain his personal feeling toward the vicious act. His responsibility was to minister to the needs of every person within the community. If he let feelings of anger and resentment take control, growth within the church and relations with the community would diminish.

While looking for another parcel of land, the members of the church made a conscious effort to befriend its hostile neighbor. United in a common cause the church and pastor grew in spiritual strength and closeness. A positive close to this story is that a larger piece of property more suitable to the needs of the congregation was found and it was here that the congregation chose to build their church.

A dominating characteristic of the three R's (reflection, re-evaluation and re-interpretation) is that they take time. Like the impatient boy who prayed, 'Lord, give me patience and please hurry,' the Christian must learn to let time take its course. The mighty oak slowly gains its strength by absorbing moisture from the earth. Regardless of how much water is poured upon the roots, they can only absorb at a given rate. Likewise, reflection, re-evaluation and re-interpretation take time.

In like manner, the content of information assimilated by the Christian leader is very important. Just as the tree which absorbs poisoned water will become ill, the believer who listens to advice from hardened men or reads material which is less than God-honoring will reflect its influence. It is no wonder that King David prayed, 'Let the words of my mouth, and the meditation of my heart, be acceptable in thy sight ...' (Psalm 19:14 - KJV).

During times of personal crisis or change, the believer may need to increase the amount of time spent in solitude and prayer. It is when a person is alone and quiet that he becomes aware of his personality, and the uniqueness of his distinction from everyone and everything else. It is this process which causes the type of growth which is characterized by depth of character and wisdom.

Sensing the tremendous task which lay before him, Nehemiah spent four months of uninterrupted thought before he began the physical rebuilding of the Jerusalem wall. He prayed over his vision and contemplated his actions carefully before he shared the vision of rebuilding the city with others. The proper amount of solitude played a key role in Nehemiah's success.

Too often a man or women feels that he or she is too busy to find time to 'catch up' with himself. Such people have difficulty finding time for silence and solitude. We are all victims of too much noise, too many distractions - victims of what some psychologists call 'stimulus flooding'. The farmer who is too busy to water his crops will not glean a bumper crop. The person who is too busy for prayerful thought and reflection will find this affects his spiritual harvest. For each person there is a need for privacy and time alone to get acquainted or reacquainted with our self-hood.

A healthy dose of reflection, re-evaluation and re-interpretation will help a person to understand better who he is and how to handle the complex situations which play a role in an active life.

RELATIONSHIPS WITH OTHERS

> 'Consult your friend on all things, especially on those which respect yourself. His counsel may then be useful where your own self-love might impair your judgment.'
>
> Lucius Annaeus Seneca

Interpersonal communication fulfills many functions. One of these is the process of 'talking things through' to gain a better understanding of them. The effective psychologist is not as concerned about the advice he conveys as in guiding his patients' thoughts. In this way, his patients talk through their problems and bring order from chaos. In the same way, we need to talk with others concerning the things which concern them so that they can make realistic assessments and wise decisions.

Many communications experts claim that the main purpose of talking to others is to reduce frustration. We communicate to bring order out of chaos - to make our future more predictable. People need to 'clear the fog' when confronted with difficult situations or when trying to gain a better understanding of themselves. One young couple heavily steeped in a competitive, professional environment began taking short one- and two-day mini-vacations away from their home. Sitting in their country cottage overlooking a mountain stream, nestled in among the pines, they were free from the distractions of their work, family and personal lives. As a result of this uninterrupted time, they were able to talk with one another in depth and gain a more realistic view of their situation.

The input of others can be very helpful, but it should not cut into the process of thinking a situation through. When trying to gain insight concerning oneself, one's spouse or a close friend may be able to provide gentle, helpful advice. Conversely, if they have questionable motives, are angry, dishonest or ill-informed, their advice may be damaging. Carefully scrutinizing the advice and comments of others is important.

Each person sees things from his own perspective. Sometimes a friend or spouse can view the situation in a more objective light. They know him and are interested in the best for him. They can help him to think through and evaluate a situation, enabling a more balanced perspective.

RESISTING EXCESSIVE INTROSPECTION

'But we will not boast of things without our measure,
but according to the measure of the rule
which God hath distributed to us,
a measure to reach even unto you.'
II Corinthians 10:13 (KJV)

Personal introspection is essential in order for a person to understand who he is. Without knowledge of what kind of a foundation exists, a contractor will have difficulty erecting a building. In the same way, the Christian must understand his foundational make-up before he can build a structurally sound temple of Christ. Too often, a person who is interested in developing his talents spends too much time dwelling on himself. Examining his past, he looks for clues as to why he acts or thinks as he does. Dwelling on his thoughts, emotions, qualities and future, he finds himself wrapped up in his new hobby: himself. Intense introspection such as this is often referred to as morbid introspection. Excessive concern for oneself can result in feelings of inadequacy, frustration, and depression. More than one Christian has become immobilized because he chose to concentrate entirely upon himself. The story goes that:

> 'The centipede was quite happy
> Until a frog in fun
> Said, "Pray, which leg goes after which?"
> That worked her mind to such a pitch
> She lay distracted in a ditch
> Considering how to run.'
>   William H. Cook

As in most things, a balance is needed to avert immobility. Knowledge of oneself should be tempered with a sincere concern for others. A pro basketball player on the west coast discovered that too much of his time was spent with concern about himself. His physical strength, development of skills and playing performance were each inward-centered. Privately he began to do volunteer work with handicapped children. In this way he was able to give of himself to others without expecting anything in return. He found that giving of himself to others helped him to keep his world in proper perspective.

REFUSING COMPARISON

> 'For we dare not make ourselves of the number, or compare ourselves with some that commend themselves, but they measuring themselves by themselves, and comparing themselves among themselves, are not wise.'
>
> II Corinthians 10:12 (KJV)

Of the billions of people who live in the world today, no two are exactly alike. Everyone looks different, thinks differently and acts differently. The qualities which distinguish one person from another are what gives each one personal identity.

Ephesians 4 points to the importance of these distinctions. As children of God, we should learn to be content within ourselves, building the qualities God has given to us and praising Him for what He has done for others. But many Christian men and women insist upon comparing themselves to others. Such comparison unfairly does one of two things: it either builds up or tears down. The discontent which generally results from an unfavorable comparison may lead to depression or excessive introspection.

People will never be happy if they spend their lives trying to be someone else. God created each person as a unique individual with an authentic greatness all their own. It is their personal qualities that should be developed. People waste their potential when they don't use it, or waste their energies trying to be someone else.

Every person has weak areas. These weaknesses may not be apparent to others, but they exist nonetheless. One executive who appeared to be a tall, good-looking, intelligent and talented leader shared that he could become elected to almost any position that he desired. It was being competent in that position which gave him trouble. Instead of comparing himself with natural leaders, he had a realistic understanding of his strengths and weaknesses. As a result, he was able to control the type of situation he allowed himself to become involved in and the direction of his personal growth.

Simply stated, Christian men and women should not compare themselves with others. Instead, they should accept themselves as they are, with the talents God has given them, praising God for the infinite wisdom He displayed when He '... made all the delicate, inner parts of my body, and knit them together in my mother's womb' (Psalm 139:13 - Living Bible).

REWARDS OF PERSONAL HANDICAPS

'For Christ's sake, I delight in weaknesses, in insults, in hardships, in persecutions, and in difficulties. For when I am weak, then I am strong.'

II Corinthians 12:10 (NIV)

If the truth were revealed, we would discover that each

person has some kind of handicap which trips him up or gets in his way. It may not be a physical lameness or psychological impairment, but each one has some characteristic which limits or handicaps him.

It is not uncommon for the person with average ability to envy those who appear to be 'super people'. Good-looking, talented and smart, they seem to have everything going for them. But like everyone else, these people have limitations too. These may be in the areas of knowledge, skill or innate ability. One pastor reported that the majority of the most beautiful and talented women he counseled were also the parishioners with the lowest self-esteem.

Paul was an excellent example of someone who had many talents. He also experienced an array of handicaps and situations which could have hindered him. In II Corinthians 11:24-27,30,31 he states:

Of the Jews five times received I forty stripes save one. Thrice was I beaten with rods, once was I stoned, thrice I suffered shipwreck, a night and a day have I been in the deep; in journeyings often, in perils of waters, in perils of robbers, in perils by mine own countrymen, in perils by the heathen ... in perils among false brethren; in weariness and painfulness, in watchings often, in hunger and thirst, in fastings often, in cold and nakedness. If I must needs glory, I will glory of the things which concern mine infirmities. The God and Father of our Lord Jesus Christ, which is blessed for evermore, knoweth that I lie not. (KJV)

Beatings, robberies, slanders and other perils plagued his life, but Paul was a wise man. He had a realistic view of who he was. This man adjusted to his situation. Instead of allowing defeat or discouragement to conquer him, he used each stumbling block as a stepping stone to build character and spiritual strength.

Many of Paul's perils involved personal pain beyond physical discomfort. Torn relationships, bitter words and even slander were experienced by Paul. Paul recognized the situation as it existed and assumed responsibility for his feelings and actions. He stated, 'forgetting those things which are behind ... I press toward the mark for the prize of the high calling of God' (Philippians 3:13-14 - KJV). He realized that if he let the pressures of the past or the infirmities of the day immobilize him, he would not be as effective a servant.

Infirmities, whether they be physical, psychological or emotional experiences of the past can serve as building blocks upon which we can develop spiritual strength and depth of character.

Helen Keller, for example, contracted a fever at eighteen months of age which left her both deaf and sightless. She later acknowledged, 'I thank God for my handicaps, for through them I have found myself, my work and my God.' Miss Keller learned to accept the aspects of her life which were unchangeable. She was then able to concentrate on the development and appreciation of the qualities which she did possess.

REVIEW

'Be very careful, then, how you live - not as unwise but as wise, making the most of every opportunity, because the days are evil.'

Ephesians 5:15,16 (NIV)

In the book of Proverbs we read concerning a man, 'For as he thinketh in his heart, so is he' (Proverbs 23:7 - KJV). This verse points out the importance of a person's attitude and view of the world. The person who is bitter and angry at life will have a different perspective than the one who has accepted the attributes and role which God has provided him. The overriding concept of this chapter is that men and women of God are responsible to take an objective view of who they are, accepting themselves and developing the characteristics with which they are endowed.

The process is not a simple one. It takes great pains to discover oneself and take a clear, objective view. More difficult is the process of accepting the qualities which in the past have been ignored or denied. The process of recognition and acceptance takes time. Just as rich-tasting soup stock requires hours of simmering on the back burner, so personal introspection that is profitable takes a great deal of careful contemplation, effort and time.

The assignments presented at the end of this book are designed to help men and women to take a closer look at themselves, their attitudes, qualities and handicaps. In the pages ahead we will explore in greater detail the ingredients which combine to form the unique personage of each individual. With a realistic understanding of himself, he can take the responsible position of developing the areas he believes need to be strengthened in order to carry out his role as an effective servant of God.

PERSONAL ESTEEM

PERSONAL ESTEEM - FROM A BIBLICAL PERSPECTIVE

> 'Do not think of yourself more highly than you ought,
> but rather think of yourself with sober judgment,
> in accordance with the measure of faith God
> has given you.'
>
> Romans 12:3 (NIV)

Personal esteem refers to the love and respect that a normal, healthy person has for himself. This concept is frequently misunderstood, especially in Christian circles. It is, therefore, important that we explore personal esteem from a Biblical perspective.

As we begin to grasp the concept of self-esteem, it is important to understand what it is not. First of all, it is not selfishness. In fact, it is just the opposite. Selfishness implies pride, which is an arrogant, haughty estimation of oneself in relation to others. It involves the taking of a superior position which largely disregards the concerns, opinions and desires of other people.

Such an attitude should be avoided by any child of God. In an effort to steer clear of any such form of pride, some Christians have overreacted. This reaction has resulted in an emphasis upon man's human inadequacy and worthlessness. For example, the hymn 'Amazing Grace' refers to man as a *wretch*. The familiar words from 'At the Cross' relate, 'Would He devote that sacred head for such a *worm* as I?' In the hymn 'Beneath the Cross of Jesus' the writer pens:

'And from my smitten heart with tears,
Two wonders I confess:
The wonders of his glorious love
And my own *worthlessness.*'

Man's 'spiritual' value without Christ is of course void, but God showed His love and value for him, even before he was born.

'For you created my inmost being; you knit me together in my mother's womb ... My frame was not hidden from you when I was made in the secret place. When I was woven together in the depths of the earth, your eyes saw my unformed body. All the days ordained for me were written in your book before one of them came to be.'

Psalm 139:13,15,16 (NIV)

The death of Christ for people who had not yet become part of the spiritual family of God further demonstrates the love and value He places on each person.

'For God so loved the world, that he gave his only begotten Son, that whosoever believeth in him should not perish, but have everlasting life.'

John 3:16 (KJV)

The fact that even before the creation of the earth, God chose men to be His children, demonstrates the value He gives to the lost.

'For he chose us in him before the creation of the world to be holy and blameless in his sight. In love

> *he predestined us to be adopted as his sons through*
> *Jesus Christ, in accordance with his pleasure and*
> *will - to the praise of his glorious grace, which he*
> *has freely given us in the One he loves.'*
>
> *Ephesians 1:4-6 (NIV)*

The Bible does not teach that men should abhor themselves (Galatians 5:14); it teaches that men should abhor sin (Proverbs 8:13).

The Apostle Paul had a healthy understanding of himself. In I Corinthians 15:9-10 he states:

> *'For I am the least of the apostles, that am not fit to be*
> *called an apostle, because I persecuted the church of*
> *God. But by the grace of God I am what I am: and his*
> *grace which was bestowed upon me was not in vain;*
> *but I laboured more abundantly than they all: yet not*
> *I, but the grace of God which was with me.' (KJV)*

Sinful men are not worthy to be called sons of God. Because of the redeeming blood of Christ, man is able to enter into God's royal family (Galatians 4:7). If man was worthless in God's eyes, then Christ would not have 'provided a way' (John 14:6) for man to be freed from his sin. God would not give His Son for mankind if He considered them to be of little worth.

Paul recognized his sinful past. In I Timothy 1:15 he once again refers to his wicked actions. In each case his actions are presented in the context of 'by the grace of God I am what I am' - a child of God. As a member of God's royal family, a joint heir with Jesus (Romans 8:17), and an individual carefully designed by God (Psalm 139:13-16), Paul had little choice but to declare that his worth as a person was through Christ. As did Paul, each Christian should strive for a realistic image of himself. This should not be characterized by pride but by a humble evaluation of what God has done through him. Self-esteem, a realistic self-appraisal, and humility should go together.

Self-esteem should be described as an accurate self-appraisal. This accuracy presupposes the inclusion of humility. A humble person is one who accepts his or her imperfections, sin and failures, but also acknowledges the gifts, abilities and achievements which have come from God. True humility is not refusing to acknowledge God-given strengths and abilities. What it is is a realistic appraisal of both our strengths and weaknesses and a grateful appreciation to God.

Coming from this should be the desire to develop these qualities further for the glory of God.

PERSONAL LOVE FOR OTHERS

'For, brethren, ye have been called unto liberty;
only use not liberty for an occasion to the flesh,
but by love serve one another.
For all the law is fulfilled in one word, even in this:
Thou shalt love thy neighbour as thyself.'
Galatians 5:13-14 (KJV)

The above verse is a clear illustration of a principle which can be traced throughout scripture. This principle is that men and women of the faith should have a healthy love and respect for themselves as well as for others. This is not to advocate an attitude of superiority, self-centeredness or pride. As can be demonstrated, these characteristics actually portray just the opposite. Self-love means to see ourselves as worthwhile creatures, valued and loved by God, gifted members of the family of God. We have been made in His image. We can love ourselves because God loves us.

As a child of God, the Christian should not be selfish or self-centered, nor should he hate himself. In order to be consistent with the scripture, 'Thou shalt love thy neighbor as_thyself' (Galatians 5:14 - KJV), he should appreciate and accept himself as a worthwhile person. Such principles are consistent with Paul's command in Romans 12:10, 'Be devoted to one another in brotherly love. Honor one another above yourselves' (NIV). Again in Philippians 2:1-4 we find:

If you have any encouragement from being united with Christ, if any comfort from his love, if any fellowship with the Spirit, if any tenderness and compassion, then make my joy complete by being like-minded, having the same love, being one in spirit and purpose. Do nothing out of selfish ambition or vain conceit, but in humility consider others better than yourselves. Each of you should look not only to your own interests, but also to the interests of others. (NIV)

Those who are able to think about the concerns of others above themselves are people who are not concerned with a shortage of love in their own life. The person who is not having his own needs met will need to care for his own needs before he can minister to others. The medic on the front lines of the battle field who has been injured will, of necessity, need to treat his own wound before he can effectively minister to his comrades.

One youth worker noticed that at nearly every high school retreat there was a despondent young person. Typically this adolescent was generally a junior high girl, overweight, with an unkempt appearance. She would make negative comments about the program and people. Observing this pattern over a period of several years, he learned to direct his staff to single such young people out and give them special attention. This TLC (Tender Loving Care) included an attentive and listening ear by the counselor, subliminal suggestions for improved appearance and the feeling of unconditional acceptance. This was done in an effort to help them overcome the problem of self-image and the lack of a feeling of personal worth.

This same inner need is demonstrated by people in a number of ways. A critical attitude, flamboyancy, selfishness, obnoxiousness and the need to always be the leader or the center of activity, are ways that reflect a person's need to gain the approval and attention of others.

The person who has accepted and learned to like himself does not have to seek out the attention of others. He operates under the assumption that others will notice him in due time. It's an issue they don't have to worry about. Instead, they can focus upon the activities in which they are engaged or in reaching out to others.

In one psychological study, a test was given to a class of 5th grade students. It was designed to measure their level of self-acceptance and love. The graduate student conducting the test expected the most verbal, intelligent, and by far the most dominant student, a boy, to score the highest. To his surprise, the youngster's score was one of the lowest. The child who measured the highest was a plain little girl who seemed on the surface to be extremely shy but she always had someone standing by her desk talking to her. When the children went out to play the other girls in the class wanted to play with her. When it was lunch time they ate with her and when it came time to leave for home, two of her friends ran halfway across the playground to walk with her. This little girl was at ease with herself.

When people are able to be at ease with themselves, accepting themselves and appreciating who they are, then they are free to give of themselves to others. Having met their own shortage of love, they are able to 'honor others above themselves'.

In order to gain an adequate level of self-love, people need to feel loved by someone else. This doesn't mean that everyone must like them. It means that they must feel loved and accepted, as they are, by someone who is 'significant' to them. The people who do not feel that they are of value to someone else will find it difficult to develop personal worth. Personal worth grows to the degree in which a person allows himself to believe that others, who are significant to him, loves him. If people feel that they are of little value to others, then they will have a shortage of love which they will try to fill. When someone feels worthy of another person's love, then he will be able to give himself true respect, value, and love.

Properly balanced self-love is essential before a man or woman can concentrate on giving of himself or herself to others. Christians need to be careful that they do not mistakenly think that any form of self-love is sin. Jesus did not say 'do not love yourself.' He said, 'Love thy neighbor as thyself.' Self-love in proper perspective is actually essential.

Christians who sincerely wish to touch the lives of others will need to realize their value to God. As a result, they can develop a healthy acceptance and appreciation of themselves. With this need (shortage) met, they can reach out in love to others.

PERSONAL IMAGE

> 'Never lose sight of this important truth,
> that no one can be truly great
> until he has gained a knowledge of himself.'
> Johann George Zimmerman

We have established that the image or picture that a person has of himself or herself should be realistic. The importance of this concept is stressed because this image lies at the root of most all of his or her conduct. For example, the person who thinks of himself as a fat and jovial, yet somewhat undisciplined, person will have a more difficult time losing weight than an overweight person who considers himself a thin person who is currently too heavy. Two people of equal abilities may enter into similar professions. One may consider himself a person who 'initiates new programs and gets things done'. The other may view himself as one who maintains existing programs. The result of these two people's influence on their respective professions will no doubt be different. The first will look for new ways to make a meaningful contribution to the organization's future development; the second will not.

The image that each person has of himself or herself will

have a profound effect upon the direction of his or her life. Recognition that a person's self-image plays a major part in their life direction is one of the most important discoveries of the century. If each of us is controlled by the mental picture that we develop of ourselves then we can take steps to form that picture in the most healthy way possible.

As a basic rule, the statement 'you are what you think you are' applies to each of us. Many tests have been made with groups of people in which their view of themselves was controlled. As a result of a changed image, each test revealed an accompanying change of the individuals' image of themselves.

In one study, a classroom of school students was taught that children with blue eyes were superior to those with brown eyes. As a result of this influence, the performance of blue-eyed children increased while that of the brown-eyed children decreased. When the process was reversed, the performance reversed as well.

The person who does not feel that he is capable of teaching a Sunday School class will find it difficult to be effective with such a project. If, however, he understands that he does possess the personality and intellect to begin such a project, his efforts could reap a different result.

A realistic understanding of personal capabilities rests upon an acceptance of the qualities which make each person unique. Elizabeth Kubler-Ross beautifully illustrated this uniqueness in her statement: 'Life is richest when we realize that we are all snowflakes. Each of us is absolutely beautiful and unique.' This 'uniqueness' which so accurately describes each person affects the image that a person has of himself or herself. A set of talents, abilities and other natural characteristics, coupled with the distinctive factors of each person's exposure to their social environment, results in a world view peculiar to that person.

Men and women who understand who they are as people, including their self-image, will be better able to control the type of situations they allow themselves to become exposed to. If one views himself or herself as a macho type, he or she may choose a profession which demands rough, hands-on, physical labor. On the other hand, the person who sees himself or herself as more of the 'gentle' type may be drawn toward the delicate refinement of the fine arts.

Whether a person views himself or herself as a person who is a great accomplisher or as one who produces little, as a leader of others or one who has the gift of helps, as an innovator of new ideas or one who maintains the status quo, as disciplined or lax, as godly or worldly, the image that he or she has will affect the other areas of his or her life and influence.

PERSONAL ACCEPTANCE

'Self-approbation,
when found in truth and good conscience,
is a source of some of the purest joys known to man.'
Charles Simmons

The late Ricky Nelson, son of the famed TV family Ozzie and Harriet Nelson, tells a story about returning to the spotlight after an absence of several years. He was asked to perform for a garden party. Many old friends from his high school days were scheduled to attend, and he was looking forward to the occasion. When the day arrived, he played his songs and tried to be genuinely himself, but he was not well received. As a person, he had grown and changed. His songs were different, his appearance had changed, and he had matured into an adult. Many who attended the party expected to see little Ricky again, but little Ricky was gone. He had developed into someone else.

Deeply hurt by the attitude and reception of his old acquaintances, Ricky Nelson wrote a song which he called 'The Garden Party'. In the song, he rightfully concludes that what is important is not what others think about him or expect him to be, but that he knows and accepts himself for who he is.

Many Christians find this sense of personal worth difficult to acquire. They are constantly looking for the approval of others and seem to be saying 'Your view of me is more important than my own opinion of myself.' This attitude is not healthy. Men and women who are reliant upon others for confirmation of their value have not yet developed adequate self-worth. Instead, they base their value upon the opinions of others, a phenomenon which we call *other worth*.

Other worth stems from the same basis as self-love. The person who has respect for the 'individual' that God made will properly value his or her own opinion. He or she will not *need* the approval of others. Of course, it is normal to *desire* the approval of others, but it is not healthy to *need* their acceptance.

This does not negate the principle that healthy men and women need the approval and acceptance of a *significant other*. The distinction is that there should not be a need to be accepted by everyone, only the significant other. After all, we all enjoy applause, compliments and praise. It feels good when we are recognized as special and significant. Seeking the approval of others is only unhealthy when it becomes a *need* rather than a *want*.

When people accept and respect themselves, they do not have to rely upon the approval of others. They are free to think and behave in a way in which they feel is God-honoring. This does not grant free license for thoughtless behavior. The principles pertaining to the Christian's influence upon his brother in I Corinthians 8 are still binding, but psychological ties to the need for the approval of others should be removed.

The pastor of a small suburban church appeared to be a natural leader. His physical presence and adult mannerism left little doubt that others would be inclined to follow him. Inwardly, the pastor had deep feelings of inferiority and needed the approval of others for most everything that he did. Although this initially led to increased involvement by board members and other officers as he sought their advice, he continued to demonstrate a lack of decisiveness in making choices even after some time had passed. Group and participatory decision-making became the rule. Program planning slowed, the amount of church time required by officers grew, and the confidence which accompanies strong leadership disappeared. In time, frustration and problems mounted, attendance dropped, and the pastor had to leave. If this pastor had learned to accept himself and overcome his need for the continual acceptance of others, his ministry might have flourished.

Although the feeling of inferiority can be a crippling disease, nearly everyone has it, to some degree. It has been estimated that 95 percent of all Americans feel inferior. Millions of persons are seriously handicapped because they have a strong feeling of inadequacy. These feelings are not generally based upon realistic data. Objectively, one would think that highly intelligent people are free from such feelings, but this is not the case. Studies show that highly intelligent people (130 I.Q. and above) suffer from more inferior feelings than those who measure less. Inferior feelings have little to do with a person's abilities, but are built upon the self-worth and acceptance that one has for himself.

At one of the Sunday Schools I attended as a child a young boy attended who suffered from cerebral palsy. Completely accepted by his parents, he was led to feel that he was of the same value as the other boys and girls. Living in a small community, both adults and children took special care to treat him in a special way. Mentally bright, he was able to attend school and many social functions. Today this boy is an adult, and although he is still reliant upon his parents for many of his physical and financial needs, he does not demonstrate evidence of inferior feelings. Outgoing and friendly, he has been taught that he is of value as a person and deserves the respect of both others and himself.

The base upon which an inferiority complex is either initiated or averted is in early life. The child who is told either verbally or in action that he or she is 'bad', 'naughty', 'not as *good* as someone else' or 'undeserving' will form much of his or her personality and behavioral patterns around this message, resulting in insecurity. The child's insecure behavior will cause others to dislike or reject him or her. This rejection creates insecurity, which results in more inappropriate or insecure actions, and so the cycle begins. Breaking such a cycle is a difficult and gradual process.

In order to accomplish such a change, a person's expectations must change. This can be accomplished through the expectations of others. When the child feels that he or she is expected to act differently, and this belief is reinforced by work or action, a gradual change will occur. Much of the child's personal identity, 'Who I am', is linked to pre-existing behavior. A naughty or shy boy may believe that this is his role in life. When placed in a new environment such as preschool or a grandparent's house, he may find his role altered. He may no longer be allowed to function as he did before. Realizing that others expect him to be a certain way, he may alter his actions and his view of himself. He may no longer consider himself the shy or naughty boy. Instead, he may see himself as the helpful or loving boy.

This is true for adults as well as children. A young man in mid management of a national firm felt overwhelmed by his responsibilities and the presence of the dominant personalities with which he was forced to work. Initially pegged as a poor communicator and inept administrator with little sense of follow through, some on the administrative staff determined to fire him. In a final attempt to keep him at the firm his supervisor determined to try an experiment. It was expressed to him by his supervisors that his expertise in handling details and seeing projects through to completion were his greatest strengths. The praise was made in both private conferences and publicly in front of his peers. He was given assignments which stretched his abilities in these areas. Faced with very real expectations from his superiors and a feeling that he was special, his quality of work improved. He began to expect more from himself and take the initiative needed to accomplish tasks and implement programs others were unable to perform. He soon received a much deserved raise and promotion.

The point to be emphasized through these illustrations is

that a person's expectations of himself or herself, as well as the expectations of others, play a key role in feelings of inferiority and personal worth. When the environment changes, so confidence and a healthy concentration on giving to others can also change. There may no longer be a need to dwell upon personal shortages and feelings of inadequacy.

Experience is an effective teacher. A mentally retarded child with cerebral palsy may come into contact only with people who love and appreciate him. An exceptionally athletic and bright child, on the other hand, might only be exposed to hateful people who make cruel and cutting remarks. The chance for feelings of inferiority is greater with the gifted child. Then feelings of inadequacy will cause them to dwell upon their own shortages rather than on giving to others. The filling of these shortages is a long and difficult task. This leads us back to the importance of being loved by someone who is important to us.

If a *significant other* demonstrates that they believe in a child and that the child has value, both the shortages caused by the lack of love and self-respect and the feelings of inferiority should diminish for that child.

People who need constant approval from those around them have not yet learned that their opinion is of significant value, that others care for them, and that they do not need to be fearful of losing their love and acceptance if they err in some way.

Christians should realize that as children of God they are loved as they are. They were made and put into an environment which God chose for them. God accepts them, forgives them, and loves them just as they are. The Christian is not expected to be anyone else or to behave like anyone else. If God had wanted that, he would have made them that way. We are each, of course, expected to develop our qualities, but only in accordance with our personality structure's innate qualities.

Some people are convinced of their worthlessness and, therefore, their inferiority. Many of Christ's most effective servants were people from shameful backgrounds. Mary Magdalene was a former harlot; Matthew was considered by the Jews to have sold out his people for filthy money; and Paul was a killer and persecutor of the early Christians: each would have been humanly justified in considering himself or herself as worthless and carriers of deep feelings of inferiority. Because they accepted Christ's forgiveness, they were given places of responsibility as servants of the Lord.

Designed by God (Psalm 139), we were also made in accordance to divine specifications. It is necessary that the believer accept himself. Then he, too, can be used as an effective servant of God.

There is the story of the boy who wrote a banner that he put across the wall in his room which read *I'M ME AND I'M GOOD, 'CAUSE GOD DON'T MAKE JUNK*. This child had the right idea. Designed by God, he felt free to accept himself as he was, not with the feelings of inferiority based upon the assessment of others, but with a recognition of his divine origin.

PERSONAL POTENTIAL

'Being confident of this very thing, that he which hath begun a good work in you will perform it until the day of Jesus Christ.'

Philippians 1:6 (KJV)

Each child of God was carefully molded to the specification of the Creator. Whether brown eyes or blue, bow legs or straight, the Lord provided each one with the talents, abilities and other essentials to fulfill His desire for their future.

At some point in his life the believer needs to stop and take inventory of the qualities which have been given to him or her. He or she can then consider how these can be used best for Christ. In I Corinthians 12:14 and 18 we read, 'For the body is not one member, but many ... But now hath God set the members every one of them in the body, as it hath pleased him.' (KJV)

If the Lord wants a person to possess certain qualities, He will give them to him or her. The Christian's responsibility is to recognize what these qualities are, and then develop them so that they can be used for God's glory. An executive with a mission organization tells the story of his conversation with a retired missionary. In his early 70's, the old gentleman had attentively listened to the speaker teaching on spiritual gifts. When the session ended, they were heading toward their accommodations when the aging gentleman asked, 'What do you think my gifts are?' The executive was bewildered. How could a missionary function with competency if he had little or no idea what his gifts were? A missionary for over 40 years, this man did not have the benefit of understanding his strengths and weaknesses. He was left to stumble in the dark when he could have had the aid of light.

Believers who fail to assess the qualities that God has given to them will have difficulty in learning their place in the body of Christ.

Too often, some Christians, in the name of humility, fail to recognize their potential. Others, once they have found their talents, are not satisfied or feel insignificant. But there is no place for insignificance in the Body of Christ. Every part is there for a reason and every part is useful. The person with the gift of encouragement is as important as the person with the gift of preaching. Each has its place and is necessary to the smooth functioning of the church.

God gave each Christian the tools that he or she needs in order to carry out his or her function as a part of the Body of Christ. No one lacks the necessary qualities or is insignificant to God. The Christian who says that he is willing 'if God can use him' is neglecting the basic principle that God designed each person to be used for His glory. After all if He is capable of using a rod, a jaw-bone, five small stones, a handful of oil and a little meal, five barley loaves and two fishes, can't He also use His children for His glory?

A look at the people Christ used to launch a worldwide enterprise should bring the obvious conclusion that He can and will use those who are willing to be used by Him. Jesus used prostitutes, crooks, fishermen, shepherds, soldiers and religious workers. By surrendering themselves to Christ, they learned that they could be of value to God.

The person who preaches that we are to think only 'lowly' thoughts about ourselves negates the fact that it is through man that God has chosen to work. The Christian should not hate himself. Instead he should appreciate and respect the abilities which have been entrusted to him to further the work of Christ.

Self-esteem is built upon proper self-worth. The person who is continually refining the qualities God has given to him or her should gain greater respect for himself or herself. As was mentioned in a previous chapter, Matthew 25:14-30 emphasizes the importance of personal development. Unfortunately, many Christians become complacent. Even though they may see the need for improvement, they are satisfied with the status quo. Maturing takes time and effort. One Christian speaker coyly suggested that each person should be presented with a bill for $100,000 for the use of his or her mind. If we were each required to make monthly payments on it, we probably would take better care of it. His contention is that people would have a better appreciation for themselves if they had to pay a price for that which God has given to them.

People who are not refining their potential in life can often be heard to say, 'I just want to make a living; I DON'T WANT TO CHANGE THE WORLD.' This attitude detracts from having a sense of purpose and the vitality of life that coincides with it. Individuals who are only making a living at work and refuse to get involved with their church and community will soon feel empty inside and lack purpose in life. This feeling does not build their self-esteem. Instead it tears at their value of themselves, creating a shortage in their self-worth and impairing their effectiveness in loving and ministering to others.

In order for people to maintain a healthy self-esteem, they must continually be growing and developing. Personal development will help them to understand and appreciate God-given potential. Not only is a recognition of this potential important, there must also be a system of refinement. The Lord, who has provided the basic resources, also provides a way to mold this raw material into a workable tool.

For each person, the refinement of the raw material will take a different shape. Two college students were discussing their college careers. One, satisfied with a baccalaureate, could not understand the other's felt need to invest several years and thousands of dollars to acquire a Ph.D. The other student, looking forward to receiving his doctorate someday, could not understand why his co-worker would be satisfied with *just* a baccalaureate degree. Over the course of years, both men acquired their desired degrees. Both men continued to be faithful, maturing servants of God. But their raw material developed differently. In the same way that the shape and use of pure gold does not alter its base value, a contrasting shape or function of talents does not negate the importance or value of one Christian over another. Each person must be himself or herself and mature in accordance with the personality, skills and background which God has given to him or her. If a man feels called to teach the junior age boy's Sunday School class, then this is what he should do. He should develop his skills so that he can be the most effective teacher he can be. If God calls him to be a missionary, then he should develop his skills in that direction.

A young executive who felt frustrated in his career was given a psychological test by an officer in the Human Resource Department of his firm. The written examination and following consultation revealed that the executive was trying to be like the men whom he admired most. Because his personality make-up and gifts were different than those whom he was trying to immulate, he was not achieving the same satisfaction or results. He then began to concentrate on being himself. He focused his energies on developing the potential God had given to him in a way that was natural for him. As a result, he was released from his frustration and was able to carry on a fruitful and satisfying career.

The man or woman who wishes to glorify God through his or her life should concentrate on developing his or her potential. This should be done in accordance with his or her personality. As a result, he or she will experience greater personal satisfaction, self-worth and inward peace.

PERSONAL UNDERSTANDING

OVERCOMING PERSONAL PROBLEMS

'A man cannot possibly be at peace with others
until he has learned to be at peace with himself.'
B. Russell

In order for Christians to minister most effectively to others, they must first be at peace with themselves and in fellowship with God. People who are preoccupied with their own inner conflicts will find it difficult to concentrate on the hurts and needs of others. Inner peace is possible only for those who live in harmony with their value systems.

The basis of a person's value system is a combination of many elements. The influence of parents, peers, the church, and society helps Christians to establish their value systems. As they assimilate the information received concerning acceptable behavior, attitudes and worth, they gain a potpourri of conflicting instructions. Parents may prescribe a set of rules which the child's peers abhor. The Bible teaches different values than those which are accepted by society in general. As people gather this information and sift through it, they filter out a set of values which they believe to be best for them. This fundamental process is not always a conscious effort.

For many people, the gathering and sorting of this data will cause little or no inner discord. For others, there is a tremendous pull between different ideologies and actions. As they endeavor to sort through these conflicting values, there is inner turmoil. The pastor of a small country church, for example, had always been told that his role in life was to be a preacher. After years of preparation and service, he came to the realization that he neither had a definite 'call' to the ministry, nor did he thoroughly enjoy the work. Week by week and month by month, this inner conflict grew. He was not able to feel relief from this tension until he was able to determine what his true inner values were.

A second major area which is responsible for a loss of inner peace is an action or thought which conflicts with established standards. Because this action is out of step with already existing ethics, it causes a breakdown in the person's identity and sense of values. A Christian, for example, who steals funds or who tells a blatant lie may experience such conflict. His understanding of who he is as a child of God is undermined by actions which contradict already established standards.

A third major area which may cause inner discord is the assimilation of new concepts and ideas which are not consistent with those already established. College students frequently experience this frustration. When challenged with new teaching in philosophy and life style, their 'conscience' creates inner conflict, indicating an inconsistency with established values.

Believers should know their values and be comfortable with who they are. If they have a basic understanding of themselves and have learned to accept their values and live a life that supports these values, they will be better able to avoid upsets of inner peace.

Philippians 2:4 states: 'Look not every man on his own things, but every man also on the things of others' (KJV). Freed from the need to deal with their own spiritual problems and inner tensions, people are able to deal with the needs of others.

DEPRESSION

'But they that wait upon the LORD
shall renew their strength;
They shall mount up with wings as eagles;
they shall run, and not be weary; and
they shall walk, and not faint.'
Isaiah 40:31 (KJV)

Depression is not confined to a few people who are stuck away in dark attics or who have weekly visits with their psychiatrists. In fact one out of every eight Americans can be expected to require treatment for depression in his lifetime. It is estimated that in any one year between four and eight million are depressed to the extent that they cannot effectively function at their jobs or they seek some kind of treatment.

Mild depression can be a part of any person's life. Disappointments, the aftermath of an important event, poor physical health, lack of sleep, diet, medication, severe personal loss, or even a chemical imbalance due to biological or glandular malfunctions, lower one's spirits.

A frequent suggestion is that depression is the result of sin. Although a conflict between a person's values and actions or unresolved anger can lead to depression, they are not always contributors. Great men of the faith have been known to suffer from depression. Charles Haddon Spurgeon, one of the world's greatest and most successful preachers reportedly stated, 'I am subject to depression of spirit so fearful that I hope no one of you ever get to such extremes of wretchedness as I go to personally, I have often passed through the dark valley (of depression).'

Other men of God who experienced depression include Moses (Numbers 11:10-16), Elijah (I Kings 19:1-18), and Jonah (Jonah 4:1-11). Depression can be the result of sin, but this is not always the case.

Sometimes depression can be the most healthy response to a situation. Many times it is simply a normal reaction to what is happening to a person psychologically or physically. Depression is a scream telling a person that something is not right and a change is needed.

One young executive, for example, accepted a position in another part of the country. Upon his arrival, he noted many social and cultural differences. People ate different foods, used different word pronunciations and colloquialisms, dressed differently, lived in a different type of housing, and even their reasoning was different. Embarking upon a new type of ministry, he faced challenges with difficulties far exceeding his expectations. Long days left little time for sleep. At the same time, he was on a restricted diet. Away from familiar surroundings, family and friends, he often faced loneliness. He was a prime target for depression. After seeking help he gained an accurate understanding of the stress which he had placed upon his physical and emotional well-being. As a result his periods of minor depression eased. A well-balanced diet, plenty of sleep, meaningful social interaction and the stability of a new home were parts of the conscious effort he took to ease the stress which was innate to his situation.

I Kings 18 and 19 describe the circumstances surrounding Elijah's depression. He had just experienced a tremendous triumph over the prophets of Baal. Hearing the disappointing message that Jezebel was planning his death, he fled into the wilderness. The letdown after his triumph, the fear of harm, the flight into the wilderness and lack of nourishment or sleep left him both physically and emotionally exhausted. A day's journey into the wilderness, Elijah 'sat down under a juniper tree: and he requested for himself that he might die; and said, "It is enough; now, O LORD, take away my life ..." ' (I Kings 19:4 - KJV).

The Lord knew what was required to restore Elijah to sound physical and mental health. First, the Lord ministered to Elijah's physical needs. 'And as he lay and slept under a juniper tree, behold, then an angel touched him, and said unto him, "Arise and eat" ' (I Kings 19:5 - KJV). Elijah continued to eat and sleep until his body was restored.

Physically able, he then embarked on a long walk. Traveling in solitude for 'forty days and forty nights' (I Kings 19:8 - KJV), he had time to meditate upon his plight. Submerged in gloomy spirits, he thought through the situation which he believed caused his condition. Wallowing in self-pity will make the situation worse, but with careful contemplation the situation at hand can be sorted out and understood.

After his careful contemplation, Elijah was given an opportunity to share his feelings of anxiety and despair. In verse 10 he states, 'I, even I only, am left; and they seek my life, to take it away' (I Kings 19:10 - KJV). This was an important exercise. When troubled or confused, it is necessary to express the situation to someone else. Regardless of whether or not they respond with good advice, there is an opportunity to put one's thoughts in a systematic or logical order.

The Lord then showed his greatness to Elijah:

'And he said, Go forth, and stand upon the mount before the LORD. And, behold, the LORD passed by, and a great and strong wind rent the mountains, and brake in pieces the rocks before the LORD ...' (I Kings 19:11 - KJV).

Being caught up in concern for one's self often causes one to forget the greatness and assistance of God. The Lord desires that His children are healthy in spirit. As our Father, He works to take care of us. II Chronicles 16:9 reads, 'For the eyes of the LORD run to and fro throughout the whole earth, to show himself strong in the behalf of them whose heart is perfect toward him.' (KJV)

With his mind centered on God, Elijah was ready to listen. The Lord showed Elijah that his situation was not as bad as he had imagined. The Lord showed him that he was not alone. 'Yet I have left me seven thousand in Israel, all the knees which have not bowed unto Baal, and every mouth which hath not kissed him.' (I Kings 19:18 - KJV)

In addition to comfort and strength from God, Elijah was given companionship. Knowing Elijah's need for the fellowship of others, the Lord told him to anoint Elisha 'to be prophet in thy room' (I Kings 19:16 - KJV). This required that Elijah spend a great deal of time with Elisha, preparing him for the ministry which he would someday have.

The Lord also gave him an assignment.

And the LORD said unto him, Go, return on thy way to the wilderness of Damascus: and when thou comest, anoint Hazael to be king over Syria: And Jehu the son of Nimshi shalt thou anoint to be king over Israel: and Elisha the son of Shaphat of Abel-meholah shalt thou anoint to be prophet in thy room. (I Kings 19:15-16 - KJV)

Elijah acted responsibly by faithfully carrying out the assignment given to him. Verse 19 reads:

So he departed thence, and found Elisha the son of

Shaphat, who was plowing with twelve yoke of oxen before him, and he with the twelfth: and Elijah passed by him, and cast his mantle upon him.

This final step is important in overcoming depression. Christian men and women may talk about their problems and pray about them, but if they do not take appropriate action to solve their problems, they will not be able to overcome them. A mature Christian needs to insure that he is taking full responsibility for his feelings. Often people claim that they are victims of circumstance. Statements such as, 'I just feel angry,' 'Her remark embarrassed me,' or 'I can't help the way I feel' demonstrate the concept of helplessness. Responsible people will respond differently. Their response might be something like, 'I have decided to be angry,' 'I've embarrassed myself,' or 'I've chosen to be upset.' Thomas Jefferson noted this concept in his *Rules of Living*. He suggested a very practical method for controlling the feeling of anger: 'When angry, count to ten before you speak; if very angry, a hundred.'

Mature Christians take responsibility for their feelings. Elijah obeyed God's instructions. Instead of reacting to the threats of Jezebel, he stepped out and took action. As a result, he was loosened from the grip of depression and was able to carry out a meaningful and productive ministry.

Depression is a complex subject, and lengthy volumes have been written about it. In these few pages, I have endeavored to highlight the natural process involved in dealing with it. Christians should realize that it is neither a sin nor a disgrace to feel gloomy, but they should not dwell upon those things which perpetuate depression or avoid the process of working it through.

STRESS

> 'Humble yourselves, therefore, under the mighty hand
> of God, that he may exalt you in due time: Casting all
> your care upon him; for he careth for you.'
>
>   I Peter 5:6,7 (KJV)

Mental and emotional disturbances are ever present in
Western society. One out of every ten Americans, according
to the United States Institute of Mental Health, suffers from
some kind of emotional or mental imbalance. One-half
million Americans are in mental hospitals. Ten million
Americans are classified 'mentally ill', and more than
250,000 are admitted each day into mental hospitals for
treatment. According to Dr. Harvey Lifsey, a Christian
counselor, 25% of all Americans will have a crisis sometime
in their life which will be too large for them to handle alone.

Mental stress and imbalance show themselves in physical
symptoms as well. Illness such as peptic ulcers, migraine
headaches, hypertension, bronchial asthma, colitis and
rheumatoid arthritis typically have psychosomatic origins.

Mental stress and imbalance are innate to Western culture,
and Christian men and women are not immune. Moods change,
high expectations lead to disappointments, and tight schedules
and personal or business problems lead to overloads: all causing
stress. The mind, just like the body, reacts to its environment.
If a person maintains a poor diet, it is inevitable that he will
become ill. If a person is exposed to a mentally unhealthy
environment, he should expect a psychological reaction.
Proverbs 18:14 states, 'The spirit of a man will sustain his
infirmity; but a wounded spirit who can bear?' (KJV)

In an effort to maintain a healthy mental state, the Christian must understand his or her inner self and those things which lead to emotional imbalance. Some people feel that their inability to master their moods means they are not healthy. Others feel that they are not spiritual if they feel depressed or sad. On the contrary, emotions *should* vary. Body cycles, exercise, medication, glands and blood chemistry all have an effect upon the emotions and reaction to stress. When offered coffee, one elderly gentleman recently declined, stating, 'The rest of the world does everything wrong when I drink coffee.' This man understands that caffeine affects his temperament, and he responsibly avoids indulgence.

Progressing toward his late-forties, one business executive noticed a gradual change in his moods. A visit to his doctor revealed a hormonal imbalance common for men going through mid-life change. Daily medication corrected this physiological imbalance and the stress he previously experienced was gone. Once again he felt like 'himself.'

Many churches give the impression that when people become Christians, their problems and the stress of life will cease. As a result, when converts have a problem, they are afraid to share it with others. Paul wrote that God 'comforteth us in all our tribulation, that we may be able to comfort them which are in any trouble, by the comfort wherewith we ourselves are comforted of God' (2 Corinthians 1:4 - KJV).

Church should be a place where people come to comfort one another and to be comforted through stressful situations. If a deacon or other leader experiences emotional stress, he should not be afraid to seek help. King Solomon advised, 'Counsel in the heart of a man is like deep water; but a man of understanding will draw it out' (Proverbs 20:5 - KJV). When Christians recognize that they have a problem, they should seek the counsel needed to work it through.

Even the finest of Christians are not exempt from the stress of personal problems. The pressures of marriage, raising children, finances, physical health and ministry all contribute to the potential of personal problems. A chaplain reportedly posted a sign on his door which read, 'If you have worries, come in and let's talk them over. If not, come in and tell me how you do it.'

Not everyone has problems which mount to the extent that they need professional help, but each person experiences stress. A person should not be afraid to admit that he has problems, especially to himself. Problems do not demonstrate a lack of spirituality; they show the need to find a way to deal with a particular situation. Peter admonishes us, telling us that the answer is, 'Casting all your care upon him; for he careth for you' (I Peter 5:7 - KJV). If spiritual men and women did not have occasional anxieties, these words would not have needed to be written. Because, as changing people, Christians encounter new and/or difficult circumstances, they may occasionally need to seek counsel.

ANXIETY

'Therefore do not worry about tomorrow,
for tomorrow will worry about itself.
Each day has enough trouble of its own.'
Matthew 6:34 (NIV)

Worry is one of the greatest killers in the Western culture. It is reported that Dr. Charles Mayo once said that half of all the beds in our hospitals are filled by people who worried themselves into them. Some noted authorities consider Dr. Mayo's estimation to be low. As mentioned earlier, mental stress or imbalance will often manifest themselves in physical symptoms. If a part of good stewardship is taking care of oneself, then Christians owe it to themselves not only to maintain good physical health, but good mental health as well.

It is of little wonder that Christ said, 'Do not worry' (Matthew 6:34 - NIV). There are many things which a Christian can worry about. Marriage, children, finances, career, neighbors, church, the list goes on.

Generally, worry will do little to help the situation. An estimated 90% of the things which people worry about never actually happen. Fear that a child might drown at the swim club will do little to help the situation. A healthy concern will lead to the presence of one or more qualified life guards, but worry after responsible precautions have been taken will only lead to unproductive anxiety and discomfort.

Moses in Exodus 14:13-14 and Jehosophat in II Chronicles 20:1-30 are examples of men who learned that they must wait upon the Lord's timing. The people who understand what they can change and what they cannot change will be able to accept their circumstances more easily. Christ taught about worry during His ministry while on earth.

In Luke 12:22-32 Jesus tells His disciples not to worry about earthly things but to concentrate on the Lord. Instead of worry, He advocates concern and mature responsibility (Luke 14:28). He also points out that worry over those things which do not have eternal value is fruitless. As God's children, 'your Father knoweth that ye have need of these things' (Luke 12:30 - KJV). Christians who are responsible in thought and action, placing the Lord in His proper place, should also have confidence that God will take care of them and their families needs.

Sincere concern can easily slip into anxiety. Excitement over the prospect of a job promotion or uneasiness about an unforeseen conflict can lead to anxiety. In Matthew 6:34 Jesus gives instruction for avoiding this. His advice is to forget about things which are to come to pass and to concentrate upon the present. Once responsible action has been taken or is being taken to prepare for the future, little else can be done. A popular saying capitalizes this concept:

> *Yesterday is a cancelled check.*
> *Tomorrow is a promissory note*
> *Today is cash in hand.*

A cancelled check is of little value except as a record of past transactions. A promissory note's value lies only in the future. Only cash in hand is of immediate usable value.

In 1913 during an address to the students at Yale University, the great physician, William Osler, shared this principle as a means to good mental health. He encouraged the students to live in 'day tight compartments' to 'shut out the dead past and the unborn future,' and thus be 'safe for today.'

At a training session for managers one educator made a helpful suggestion. He advised his audience to ask themselves what the worst possible outcome could be when troubles arose. Fear of the unknown tends to take things out of proportion, he shared. By recognizing what the worst possible outcome could be, boundaries would be established and a more realistic view would result. With an understanding of the depth and consequences of a situation, practical solutions could be explored.

Problems, uncertainties and difficulties are parts of everyone's life. Through them come stability, wisdom, and maturity. By realistically confronting them and understanding full well the possible consequences, a person should be able to reach feasible solutions and ease his inner tensions.

Philippians 4:6-9 provides careful guidelines for dealing with anxiety. Verse 6 states, 'Be careful for nothing; but in everything by prayer and supplication with thanksgiving let your requests be made known unto God' (KJV). Paul commands the Christian not to worry. The believer is summoned to 'let (his) requests be made known unto God.' The release of anxieties may not be easy. Although prayerful concern is natural, a person is likely to turn his attention away from the Lord to dwell upon the distress when concern turns into anxiety. If the problem is turned over to the Lord, the need for change decreases and tensions diminish. The Christian's attention can then be placed toward God.

In II Chronicles 20:1-30, Jehosophat was confronted with the threat of a seemingly hopeless battle. Acknowledging sure defeat, he turned to God in prayer. The Lord said to him, 'Be not afraid or dismayed by reason of this great multitude; for the battle is not yours, but God's' (verse 15 - KJV).

Confident in the promise that the will of the Lord would be served, 'Jehosophat bowed his head with his face to the ground: and all Judah and the inhabitants of Jerusalem fell before the LORD, worshipping the LORD' (verse 18 - KJV). The next morning, before the impending battle, he demonstrated his trust in the promise of God. 'He appointed singers unto the LORD, and that should praise the beauty of holiness, as they went out before the army, and to say, Praise the LORD; for his mercy endureth forever' (verse 21 - KJV).

A man of faith, he placed his trust in the Lord. Having done his part, he placed his confidence in the wisdom and promises of God.

Philippians 4:7 describes the promise made to the believer who turns his cause for distress over to the Lord: 'And the peace of God, which passeth all under-standing, shall keep your hearts and minds through Christ Jesus' (KJV).

The promise was realized in the life of Jehosophat. When he first learned of the impending battle he 'feared' (II Chronicles 20:3). After he turned the situation over to God, he was at peace and even 'appointed singers unto the LORD' (vs. 21 - KJV). Marching onto the battleground singing praises of triumph was a strong sign of confidence in the Lord.

A missionary intent on starting a church tells of being afraid to canvas a community. He dreaded the idea of knocking on doors because of the possibility that people might reject him. Nervously, he proceeded with his assignment. Stumbling through his presentation, his actions reflected his fear, and he was not well-received. When he turned his anxiety over to God, this young man relaxed. He no longer focused on the fear of personal rejection. Instead he prayerfully acknowledged the importance of sharing with others about Christ. As a result, he gained inward peace and was able to visit others with a decreased fear of rejection.

Philippians 4:8 points to a third important action to be taken by the believer. It states:

Finally, brethren, whatsoever things are true, whatsoever
things are honest, whatsoever things are just, whatsoever
things are pure, whatsoever things are lovely, whatsoever
things are of good report; if there be any virtue, and if
there be any praise, think on these things. (KJV)

The thoughts and meditations of a worried person will
largely determine the degree of the anxiety. If he frets and
fusses about an impending event, the trauma will rise out of
proportion. Concentration on the Lord and those things
which represent a righteous life will most likely keep concern
in balance. When schemes, revenge or wrongdoing are
replaced with a truthful, honest approach, the Christian
maintains his integrity and the Lord is glorified.

One Church Planting Missionary, for example, worked
very hard to build spiritual depth and increase numbers at one
of his mission points. He developed close ties with the
church leaders. The ministry finally matured to the point to
where it was ready to take on the support of a full-time pastor.
Assisting in the selection of what seemed to be 'God's man',
the church commissioned their first pastor. Of necessity, the
minister's salary was low. He had a large family. Unknown
to the missionary, the pastor, desiring a new car, borrowed
some money from one of his parishioners. From another he
acquired funds for some electronic equipment; and from
another money for a special project. When the notes came
due the minister was unable to honor them and tensions grew.
The missionary was called to the scene. With much prayer
the missionary turned the situation over to God. He felt it was
God's battle and not his. Considering himself only an
instrument of God, he tried to reconcile this difficult situation,
but to no avail. His concern was for the spiritual welfare of

both the pastor and the congregation. Confronting them with reason and scripture, he sought to bring them together to work a mutually agreeable and virtuous solution.

It was with a heavy heart that the missionary opened the annual business meeting. The building was filled to capacity as the head deacon marched forward, stated his case against the pastor, resigned as deacon and left the room. In mass, most of the people followed. Although the missionary was hurt and disappointed, he continued to place the situation in God's hands. Knowing that he had faithfully done his part, he refused to worry about the future or to dwell on past regrets. Instead, he relied upon the Lord for strength. After the incident was over, the missionary set his sights upon the spiritual health of the community and pastor.

The missionary worked with the pastor to provide personal, family and spiritual council. The pastor moved away from the area and later became active as a layman with another congregation. He secured secular employment and over time repaid his debts.

With his integrity intact the missionary also set about rebuilding relationships in the community, praying for individuals hurt by the situation and maintaining church services. After a period of time the mission point regained its former strength and called another full-time pastor.

Had the missionary worried and become angrily frustrated with the situation and the people involved, rather than dwelling upon those things which were 'honest, just, pure and virtuous', the immediate consequences would have been more severe. The long-term effect upon the community, and the missionary himself would have been more painful.

Jehosophat, too, placed his thoughts upon God and those things which would bring the best result to his people. He was not concerned about conquering his enemies and the spoil which he could gather. He was concerned about the safety and welfare of God's chosen people.

Philippians 4:9 points to a final action to be taken, 'Those things, which ye have both learned, and received, and heard, and seen in me, do: and the God of peace shall be with you.' (KJV)

In II Chronicles 20, Jehosophat not only listened to God, he accepted the Lord's promise and dwelt upon righteousness, taking the appropriate action. Verses 17 and 20 read, '... fear not, nor be dismayed; tomorrow go out against them: for the LORD will be with you ... And they rose early in the morning, and went forth into the wilderness of Tekoa' (KJV). The king had confidence in the instruction of God, and he did what he had been instructed to do. He knew that what he was doing was right. As a result, he had such peace that he slept soundly the night before the battle.

At the church described earlier, the missionary took the steps which he knew were right. He did not just sit back and hope that the situation would resolve itself. He took the responsible action that he believed was necessary to resolve the situation. Even though the immediate results were not ideal, he had peace in knowing that he acted in a way which was right. It was this peace and the resulting personal integrity which allowed him to continue to minister in the community and guide the church toward renewed growth.

Areas of concern are a part of any person's life. For a parent, afternoon naps and well-balanced meals show a responsible concern for a small child's health. At Sunday School, adult supervision insures that scissors will not be used in a harmful way and the lesson is presented as accurately as possible to guide the student toward correct understanding. Concern creates a desire for responsible behavior, but too much caution can lead to needless worry and anxiety. The scriptures teach responsibility, limiting the amount of concern.

ACHIEVING PERSONAL HAPPINESS

> 'I came that they may have and enjoy life, and have it in abundance - to the full, till it overflows.'
>
> John 10:10 (Amplified)

What is Happiness?

The American humorist Charles M. Schultz says that 'Happiness is a warm puppy'. Ira U. Cobleigh describes it as 'a stock that doubles in a year'. Realistically, yet philosophically, Thomas S. Szasz characterizes happiness as,

'an imaginary condition formerly often attributed by the living to the dead, now usually attributed by adults to children and children to adults.'

Happiness means different things to different people. Some people look at it as exuberant joy and elation, while others see it as a subtle yet pleasant peace which indwells the inner soul. For our purpose, we will use the latter of these two definitions. Although exuberance and elation are often part of happiness, they are not essential. Personal calamity, such as the death of one's child, may result in the need for sorrow. A mentally healthy person will be able to experience sorrow in the context of a 'pleasant peace'.

Cycle of Emotions

Psychological health requires that people experience both high and low feelings. A healthy person is capable of experiencing a full range of human emotions. The old southern spiritual, 'Nobody Knows De Trouble I've Seen,' describes the experience of most people.

> *'Sometimes I'm up.*
> *Sometimes I'm down,*
> *O, yes, Lord.*
> *Sometimes I'm almos' to de groun'*
> *O, yes, Lord.'*

The Christian should recognize that he goes through normal cycles. The saying that 'all sunshine makes a desert' is valid. Variety is the keynote for an active life. Routine can breed boredom, complacency, discouragement, and depression. The natural cycle of changing moods presents a need for change. If such changes are not in excess, they provide a part of man's natural make-up.

Who is responsible for your Happiness?

Epictetus, the Greek slave, wrote, 'If a man is unhappy, his unhappiness is his own fault.' This saying is built upon the presupposition that man was originally created by God to be happy. Philippians 4:4 commands the believer to 'Rejoice in the Lord always: and again I say, Rejoice' (KJV). The intent is that the believer can and must rejoice under all circumstances, regardless of what they are (Philippians 4:11) with the attitude that 'This is the day which the LORD hath made; we will rejoice and be glad in it' (Psalm 118:24 - KJV).

Paul's mind-set was that despite the circumstances, he

would appreciate them as they were. When in prayer with his fellow Christians, he rejoiced over the fellowship and encouragement. When in prison, shipwrecked or tired after a long journey, he joyfully appreciated the Lord's presence in these circumstances. He saw each situation as an opportunity for him to bring honor to God. Paul could still experience the feeling of sorrow and discouragement, but these emotions were accepted within the overall context of a healthful and happy attitude toward life.

Each day, Paul set the stage for a joyful outlook. In Ephesians 4:23 he writes, 'and be constantly renewed in the spirit of your mind - having a fresh mental and spiritual attitude' (Amplified). He approached life from a viewpoint of acceptance and appreciation for Christ.

Building upon this attitude, he writes in Philippians 4:8:

'Finally, brothers, whatever is true, whatever is noble, whatever is right, whatever is pure, whatever is lovely, whatever is admirable - if anything is excellent or praiseworthy - think about such things' (NIV).

By dwelling upon those things which are good, Paul was able to perpetuate his attitude of thanksgiving to and joy in God.

The believer who sets his mind on those things which are pure and righteous will face life with a foundation upon which to happily rejoice in the Lord, regardless of the circumstances.

Happiness necessitates a balance between vocation and avocation

The concept that a person should be happy and 'rejoice in the Lord always' has not always been popular in the American culture. The early Puritans were pious people, not known for being jovial. They emphasized sacrifice, hard work, temperance and worship. Recreation and relaxation, except for Sabbath rest, were frowned upon.

In contrast, many modern-day Christians seem caught in the trap of believing that as a child of God they should always be on an emotional or spiritual 'high'. Because work often denotes a difficult or unpleasant task, they may shy away from it. The concept that work necessitates unhappiness is based upon a false premise. Although some types of work may be unpleasant for certain types of individuals, people, especially in the professions, often become caught up with the vision they have for their work and thus find happiness and peace of mind in their vocation.

The difference between work and play is a mind-set. What may be work for one person is the avocation of another. The person whose time is concentrated on working with people, teaching and study may find that time spent working in his garden or on his car is relaxing. In contrast, the machinist, farmer or mechanic may find that the week night Bible class and Sunday service provides the pleasant uplift he needs in his avocation.

For some people, their work is both their vocation and their avocation. Their friends, personal ministry, family and professional goals are each related to their work. The desire to do anything else with their time is minimal. The saying, 'Work is play, play is work, that is all you need to know' well describes their life. For them, personal and spiritual fulfillment is found in their profession. Because the difference between work and play is a mind-set, they have learned to enjoy their occupation to the degree that it becomes their play.

One minister, for example, describes his family as a ministry family. Each member takes part in the church. Teaching Bible Club and Sunday School, playing the piano, helping out at camp, arranging craft projects, sweeping out the church and even washing pots and pans are parts of the duties of the children. The father is heavily involved in overseeing the work of the church, handling unforeseen crises, teaching, and preaching and running the summer program. His wife teaches at Bible School and camp, performs the unpleasant tasks which church members hesitate to volunteer for, and constantly has her home available for entertaining. From morning until night the family's conversation centers around their ministry.

Even though people may love their work and ministry, time away from the pressures associated with it are a psychological and physical must. A change of pace and environment will actually increase productive potential. Play, separate from one's vocation, if even in small doses, is necessary. Play is re-creative because it seems to add something to a person. It's like an investment in oneself. Even when the activity is physically exhausting, we feel fuller, more complete, than before. The play principle here is similar to the one that is applied to the love relationship where giving of oneself produces the feeling of receiving. As we allow ourselves to play, we receive an increase in our capabilities and our perception of who we are. This restores and re-energizes us. Play is recreative and a necessary part of developing to our greatest potential.

Many people who are vitally engrossed with their jobs have found numerous ways to get away from their work for some recreation. One executive purchased a camping trailer which he and his wife regularly take into the nearby mountains for overnight outings. Another uses a mountain cabin owned by one of his workers. Others work in their yard, play golf, mountain climb or even fish.

In Ecclesiastes 3:1-8 King Solomon states that there is a time for everything. The man or woman who wishes to be a happy, healthy and productive servant of God will search out and find the type of recreation and proper balance of activities which are right for him or her.

Happiness comes from Giving

Barring physical illness, excessive stress or other such variables, the root of happiness stems from the responsible, self-directed act of giving. In Romans 15:2 we read:

> *Let each one of us make it a practice to please (make happy) his neighbor for his good and for his true welfare, to edify him - that is, to strengthen him and build him up spiritually. (Amplified)*

A quick look at the people who are considered to be happy will reveal people who have learned to literally forget about themselves and concentrate upon the needs of others. For example, two Christian professionals had businesses which were situated close to one another. Both had equal training, similar background and almost mirror-like occupations, but they were at the opposite ends of the scale when it came to happiness.

One was very protective of his personal time. Under the guise that his family came first, he refused to make any special effort to meet with people when it fit their schedule. He spent only a minimal number of hours on the job activities and constantly complained about his financial condition.

Unprepared, he provided less than adequate care for his clients and yet played several rounds of golf each week.

The other person gave unselfishly of his time and energy to his clients. His constituents knew that he was available to them at any time and that what was his was theirs. Intensely concerned with helping people, he listened to their needs, prayed with them and assisted them in whatever way he could. Because of his vision and sensitivity, his business mushroomed and he displayed an affect of happiness and contentment.

As the unhappy professional looked at the growing work of his unselfish friend, his interest was not that he might learn to be more effective. His concern was that he might look bad because his business was regressing while his friend's was growing. Their mutual acquaintances perceived clearly which man was filled with symptoms of unhappiness and which one was not. The saying, 'Happiness is a perfume you cannot pour on others without getting a few drops on yourself' accurately describes the principle presented here.

A story which further illustrates this point involves a little cat which was chasing its tail. A big cat sat contently by, watching. He asked, 'Why are you chasing your tail?' The kitten replied, 'I have learned that the best thing for a kitten is happiness, and that happiness is in my tail. Therefore, I am chasing it; and when I catch it, I shall have happiness.' The wise old cat responded, 'I too have paid attention to the wisdom of the world and have learned that happiness is in my tail. I have further noticed that whenever I chase after it, it keeps running away from me but when I go about my business, it seems to follow me wherever I go.'

Jesus said:

'If anyone would come after me, he must deny himself and take up his cross and follow me. For whoever wants to save his life will lose it, but whoever loses his life for me and for the gospel will save it.' (Mark 8:34, 35 - NIV).

Jesus also said, 'I am come that they might have life, and that they might have it more abundantly' (John 10:10 - KJV). Christ's intent was to provide an abundant life for everyone. The method for acquiring this abundant life includes giving of oneself through spiritual readiness, self-discipline and concern for others.

The Christian who wishes to live a happy and peaceful life in Christ must first realize that happiness is more than elation. It is a deep, inner peace which results, not just from external circumstances, but from a right relationship with God, healthful appropriation of time and concern for people outside of oneself.

'But when the Holy Spirit controls our lives He will produce this kind of fruit in us: joy, peace, patience, kindness, goodness, faithfulness, gentleness and self-control ...' (Galatians 5:22-23 - Living Bible)

DETERMINING PERSONAL VALUES

'Naked came I from my mother's womb,
and naked shall I return thither:
the LORD gave, and the LORD hath taken away;
blessed be the name of the LORD.'
Job 1:21 - KJV

Values are those things which are important to an individual.
A child may place a great deal of worth in a toy or pet. An
adult may treasure his family or job. What is deemed to be
of worth by one person may not seem to be of value to
another. It is in this sense, values serve as guides in
determining a person's actions. The man who places a great
deal of worth upon his family relationship will focus his
energies and time in that direction. If his career or hobby
takes greater precedence, his energies will be concentrated in
that area.

One pastor tells how he discovered the *true* direction of
his values. Serving as the leader of a growing ministry, he
found himself involved in extensive counseling as well as
administrative and teaching responsibilities. He enjoyed
counseling and therefore decided it would be good to open
a counseling center. As this new ministry grew, so did the
number of hours required to insure its operation. From early
morning until late into the evening he nurtured this
demanding ministry. On a particular memorable morning his
secretary called his office and informed him that there was
a young lady in the foyer to see him. He replied that he was
booked for the rest of the day and asked if she would please
make an appointment. His secretary emphasized that this
particular person had a problem of parental neglect. She
thought the situation needed immediate attention. Would he
at least see her for a few minutes? Somewhat disquieted, he
replied that he would see her, but only because it was an
emergency.

Engulfed in updating notes from his previous
appointment, he failed to look up from his desk as she entered
the office. When he finally looked up from his papers, he
found himself staring directly into the eyes of his own

daughter. Humbled, he asked for her forgiveness and cancelled his appointments. He spent the rest of the day with his daughter.

This was a hard lesson to learn. The pastor had thoughtlessly placed his ministry before his family. With this as his value base, the rest of his time and energies were situated around it.

Men and women of God should advocate a holistic approach to values. *Holistic* refers to the whole or entire person. This includes physical, social, cultural, family, spiritual, mental and ministry values. When each area has been scrutinized as to the amount of emphasis, time and effort that should be placed on it, a person will adjust the priorities so they come into proper balance.

Many of the things which people cherish are basic and form the foundation upon which they build the rest of their values. These can be called 'primitive values'. Other things are not as important and are built upon these foundational or primitive values. Such supported endearments are called 'secondary' or 'inconsequential' values. Primitive values are fundamental. They are universally accepted by the people who live in a particular society. Morals, standards, right or wrong behavior, respect for life, fidelity and possessions are parts of the fundamental base upon which other values and actions are built.

When there is a violation between what people hold as primitive beliefs and their actions, their entire value structure is in danger. Acting within the scope of their primitive system is therefore important for people's mental health.

For Christians, the Bible provides a set of standards. With this as their guide (primitive values), they can establish secondary or inconsequential standards. A primary value may be that Christians provide adequate shelter for their families. If this is not established, they will experience tremendous inner stress. A related secondary value would be the type of housing provided. For example, some people feel a mobile home or apartment is satisfactory. Others prefer a cape cod or ranch style house. A home's location may also be important. Some people feel comfortable in the hustle and bustle of the city while other people prefer the solitude of a rural area. Although a person's secondary values may be important, they are not primary if they do not constitute the basic foundation upon which the person determines his personal identity and basic behavioral patterns.

The school teacher may believe that one brand of curriculum is better than another. If a school decides not to use material from that publisher, the teacher may not agree with their decision, but if the curriculum is fundamentally sound, it should be of little importance to his total value system or his relationship with the people at the school.

Repeatedly we emphasize the individual qualities of each person. Just as each one is made with particular talents, skills and other characteristics, so he or she is developed in a special way. Each of his or her personal qualities influence the way in which he or she perceives the world and the system of standards given to him or her. It is, therefore, important that each person learn the values which are right for him or her.

Two Christian men discussed the differences in their life styles. Both were equally effective in their jobs, active in their churches and committed to their families, but their personal standards required a somewhat different formula for a healthy balance.

Mr. 'A' drove an older car which looked rugged and had been overhauled several times. He lived in an older home which needed paint. Ragged furniture added to the lived-in look which resulted from the clutter of things not being picked up. His wife chose not to work outside the home but to concentrate her time on raising their children.

Mr. 'B' drove a new car which was always kept clean. He lived in a modest modern home which was complemented by contemporary furniture and a clean appearance. His wife chose to work outside the home, developing professionally and helping to provide financially.

Each man felt that he was living in a life style which was balanced and healthy for him. Mr. A enjoyed having his wife at home and the comfortable feeling of being able to put his feet on the coffee table. Mr. B would not have been comfortable in these surroundings. Though not fastidious, he felt uncomfortable with clutter and believed that everything should be in its place.

Depending upon his or her own personal needs and preferences, each person should decide on standards for each area of his or her life. He or she should then strive to establish and live within the boundaries of these standards. This includes the amount of time spent in prayer and Bible study, quality family time, the scope of his ministry, financial needs, personal and professional development, and time spent with his or her spouse.

The book of Proverbs emphasizes that it is important for each believer to establish a healthy balance. Proverbs 30:8,9 reads:

'... give me neither poverty nor riches; feed me with food convenient for me: Lest I be full, and deny thee, and say, Who is the LORD? or lest I be poor, and steal, and take the name of my God in vain' (KJV).

More than one person has been greatly troubled over his or her lack of finances. Dwelling upon those things which cannot be acquired is easy for the person who desires to provide a good, healthy life for his family. A healthy balance is evident when the amount of concern over the 'have nots' is minimal. Excessive conversation and thought about the material things which one does not possess will not enhance one's relationship with God. Spiritual maturity and a healthy assessment of needs are necessary before Christians can determine the emphasis to place in each area of their lives. Stated on the bulletin board in the kitchen of one Christian couple is a saying designed to help them maintain a proper perspective of their priorities. It reads, 'The most important things in life arn't things.'

A healthy, balanced life will allow for growth and comfort spiritually, socially, financially, personally and domestically. As children of God, each Christian man and women should strive to bring honor and glory in all that he or she says and does.

PERSONAL GROWTH

RESPONSIBILITY FOR GROWTH

> 'Begin to be now
> what you will be hereafter.'
>   St. Jerome

In the preceding chapters, foundational information was presented which is designed to help a person form a basic understanding of his personal make-up. The following pages will dwell upon the process involved in developing the basic raw materials provided by God. Directed personal growth requires planning, patience and persistence. The Christian who leaves his personal development to the haphazard influences of chance may mature in areas which will not necessarily enhance his or her ministry, family or spiritual walk. An individually designed, systematic process will better insure both the direction and the pace of improvement.

In 1964, Margaret Mead, the famed anthropologist, estimated that the average healthy human being is functioning at 10 percent of capacity. Since that time, her colleagues have estimated that we are operating at between 2 and 4 percent of capacity. This change in perception is due to the discovering that every human being has more power, resources and abilities than was suspected. The increased understanding of human potential brings to light the tremendous responsibility which man has to diligently refine himself. Such cultivation necessitates a continual process.

By design, man was left with the responsibility for his own actions (Matthew 25:14-30). He was provided with the ability to choose between right and wrong. The mature Christian will realize the tremendous responsibility which this places upon him or her. A person is held liable for the process of growth as it is cultivated in his or her life and is accountable to God for his or her actions.

Fortunately for man, God is a specialist at changing lives. The believer who allows God to take full control of his or her life, establishing a systematic program for personal growth, will surge ahead in depth and refinement. A purely self-directed program will take into account only a mortal view. God understands the total person, recognizing all of his or her needs as well as his or her potential. Reliance upon prayerful sensitivity to the Holy Spirit will help insure a wholesome plan.

The story is told of a man who always boasted about being self-made. A disgusted acquaintance of his finally came up with this reply: 'If, as you say, you are self-made, you certainly relieve the Lord of a lot of embarrassment!' Reliance upon the Lord is essential if the ultimate result is to bring honor and praise to Him.

As emphasized previously in this study, God has bestowed upon each person an individually prescribed set of talents and circumstances. Some individuals will take advantage of these natural gifts, others will not. Only those who cultivate their abilities will reap a bountiful harvest.

Beethoven, though he was deaf, was a magnificent musician. Determined not to give in, he was overheard shouting at the top of his voice as he slammed both fists on the keyboard, 'I will take life by the throat.' It was because of strenuous discipline and concentration on refining his abilities that he became so productive. Diligence and hard work are two ingredients which cannot be neglected. Many seemingly untalented people cry that they would be successful if they only had the talents or background of others, but the cry-babies of life would do the same thing with someone else's talents as they are doing with their own: nothing!

Many people hide behind the great 'ifs' of life: if I were more handsome, if I were talented, if I were not handicapped, if I had money, if I came from a different family. Each 'if' represents an excuse, and neglects the fact that only one person holds responsibility for an individual's life, and that person is one's self.

Some Christians go through their entire lives blaming others or circumstances for their personal failures. Throughout scripture it is people of action who bring about changes.

Amos was called to be a prophet while a farm laborer picking sycamore fruit. What would have happened if he excused himself from service saying, I would be pleased to serve only if I had a better education. When God asked Isaiah, 'Whom shall I send and who will go for us?' Isaiah could have replied, 'You know you can always count on me, God, but the other day King Uzziah died. Now the whole nation may fall apart. We're all running a bit scared. But if our national affairs were in better shape I would be pleased to serve.' Both men had ample opportunity for excuses but they both chose to rise to the occasion and use their talents in the best way they knew how.

Joseph is an excellent example of a believer who did not fall prey to the irresponsible 'ifs' of life. Sold into Egyptian slavery by his own brothers, he maintained a strong work ethic and high moral standards. As a result, he became the overseer of Potiphar's household and possessions. Because he refused an illicit relationship with Potiphar's wife, she falsely accused him, and he was thrown into prison. While he was in jail, Joseph did not make excuses. Instead, he accepted responsibility for who and what he was. Consequently, he gained the confidence of the prison keeper and was given responsibility over all of the inmates. Few people could stand up under the perils experienced by Joseph. As a man of God, he recognized that he was responsible to 'make the most of every opportunity' (Ephesians 5:15-16 - NIV).

Men and women are ultimately responsible for the development of the qualities which God has given to them. A systematic and deliberate development program will more greatly increase their effectiveness in glorifying God than if they left their maturity to chance. On the following pages we will explore the key elements of personal growth and development. One thing must remain clear throughout this study. The ultimate responsibility for a person's development is not on anyone's shoulder but the believer himself. As Shakespeare said in *Julius Caesar*, 'The fault, dear Brutus, is not with our stars, but with ourselves ...'

FOUNDATION FOR GROWTH

'A man's mind stretched by a new idea
can never go back to its original dimensions.'
Oliver Wendell Holmes

The premise upon which this book is written is that Christian men and women are endowed with certain talents and abilities. It is their responsibility to use these talents to glorify God, and the use of these talents is based largely upon the degree and direction in which they are developed.

Man was made with the inherent need to use his gifts. Even Adam, when placed in the garden of Eden, was given duties to perform which would stimulate his body and mind. In Genesis 2:15, he is described as being the one designated to 'till' the land in the beautiful garden of Eden. In verse 19, he is further instructed to name the animals. Both Adam's body and mind were kept alert and enriched by the tasks which God assigned to him.

Certain aspects of this process need to be understood. One is that personal enrichment is a continual process for the active and lively person. The capacity for both physical and mental (cognitive) growth peaks around the age of twenty. The person who establishes a pattern of cultivating his maturity will continue to cultivate the ability God has endowed him with, whereas the person who does not will begin to deteriorate. Even at a young age, the adults who fail to remain alert find it increasingly difficult once again to discipline their minds and/or bodies if they wish to bring them back into healthful tone. The old adage that 'you can't teach an old dog new tricks' could be more accurately stated, 'You can teach an old dog new tricks, but it takes longer.' The presupposition is that an old dog has stopped learning and the process of rejuvenating this discipline is therefore difficult.

The Apostle Paul in I Timothy 4:14 states 'Neglect not the gift that is in thee' (KJV). Paul himself insured continual personal growth by remaining alert and active throughout his Christian life. Even while he was in prison, he continued to study the scripture, teach the word, correspond with his churches, and witness to those around him.

It has been stated that 'the road to success is always under construction'. The Christian who has an effective Christian life will remain alert, strive to be creative, develop a sense of urgency for the lost, enrich his or her relationship with God, and maintain physical health. In this sense, an effective Christian must be a growing Christian. As in the example of Paul, the believer should not expect to receive special recognition for continued growth. This growth should be an inherent part of his Christian walk. Clovis G. Cappell writes,

> *'The bee is not to be prized only when it does not sting. It is entitled to respect because of its honey ... the value of a rose bush is not measured by the fewness of its thorns, but by the wealth and beauty of its roses.'*

At a special training conference for teachers the speaker pointed out that personal development in any area is based upon three things. The first of these is a person's attitude. A person who states that he or she wants to teach children but who has a poor attitude about people, learning or the teaching process will not be very effective. When an alive and caring attitude is demonstrated, growth is able to take place. The second area is the acquisition of knowledge. A contagiously alert attitude will be of little value if there is not an understanding of the content to be taught. Finally, in order to become an accomplished teacher, a willing worker must develop skill. Knowledge and enthusiasm are essential, but they need to be tempered with the skillful acts of story telling and class discipline before they can be successfully used.

Each of these three items is essential before healthful growth can occur, but too great an emphasis in any one area will distort the growth. Not unlike a triangle, each side must be in perfect balance before the ideal can be accomplished.

Although an over-emphasis or neglect of one particular aspect will alter the perfection of growth, it is unlikely that true growth will reflect equal development in each of these areas at any one time. When a worker accepts the challenge to teach a Sunday School class, his enthusiasm will generally exceed his budding knowledge and skill. As years pass, the knowledge of God's word may surpass his skill in teaching. Similarly, his ability to work with a specific age or interest group may expand beyond his knowledge of the scriptures. Ideally, these three areas will grow at the same pace. Realistically, however, there will be times when the advancement of one or two areas will exceed the other. A person should take steps to remain alert to possible distortions and endeavor to insure that a healthy balance between knowledge, attitude and skill is maintained.

With such balance should come the depth inherent to true character. The person who greets everyone with a jovial smile and a warm handshake, but has developed little depth of spiritual knowledge or skill in Christian living, will be of little help to the church. Likewise, the teacher who spends many hours in Bible study, but does not feel the need to fellowship with people will be strong on knowledge, yet weak on depth of understanding. Personal development should include balanced depth and growth in each area to reach healthy balanced maturity.

Comfort Zones
Personal growth can only be accomplished when one experiences discomfort. Too often a person becomes comfortable and almost complacent with life. Year in and

year out, the same basic programs, structures and schedules are followed. The yearly routine becomes less and less of a challenge, and the personal growth involved diminishes. Each year, the same basic schedule is followed as the last. The person in this state has relaxed in what is called a 'Comfort Zone'. This Comfort Zone includes family life, social friends, theological understanding, and even the geographical perimeters of one's life.

To a degree, people need to feel comfortable in their lifestyles. Conversely, when a Comfort Zone leads to complacency, the tools with which God has endowed each of His children loose refinement. This loss will influence the extent to which their talents are developed for the glory of God.

When a person determines to enrich his or her talents he or she must step out of the Comfort Zone. The greater the increase in number and variety of new experiences, the larger the Comfort Zone. The shy recluse lives in a sheltered world with a limited Comfort Zone, limiting his or her potential. The person who systematically, 'in a fitting and orderly way' (I Corinthians 14:40 - NIV), expands his zone will increase both his or her personal and ministry potential. As stated above, once 'a man's mind (is) stretched by a new idea (it) can never go back to its original dimension' (Oliver Wendell Holmes). An expanded Comfort Zone will develop new boundaries in which the person will now feel comfortable. He will have grown beyond the dimensions of the past.

One of the purposes of this book is to help the interested believer to develop 'a fitting and orderly way' of healthfully expanding a Comfort Zone.

There are two basic motivations for developing an expanding Comfort Zone: deficiency motivation and growth motivation. *Deficiency motivation* is more common and stems from a need. The obese person may be concerned about his health and therefore begin to expand his Comfort Zone of discipline by adhering to a balanced diet and rigorous exercise. The new convert who realizes his lack of understanding of the things of Christ delves into the scriptures so that he or she can fill his or her incomplete knowledge of basic biblical truth.

Growth motivation stems from a different root. Enrichment is not the outcome of a felt need, but comes from the desire to increase rather than from a felt deficit. The person who exercises and diets under growth motivation does so to improve his physical and mental health, not because he is fat. The Christian who spends time in the scriptures should do so, not because he needs to fill a spiritual void, but because he wishes to enhance his understanding and relationship with his Lord.

As the reader of this book you will be matured by these two factors. Your goal should be to either establish, maintain or increase *growth maturation* through participation.

BLUEPRINT FOR GROWTH

'To be nobody but yourself
in a world which is doing its best day and night
to make you like everybody else
means to fight the hardest battle
which any human being can fight
and never stop fighting.'

E. E. Cummings

Everyone has a blueprint for his or her life. Whether born into a poor family isolated in the mountains or to a family of means with great exposure to culture in the city, God allows each child to be exposed to an environment which will influence the development of his or her identity. In many ways, this identity provides a 'blueprint' or 'life map' to follow. Such a blueprint can be described as a life plan, very much like a dramatic stage production that an individual feels compelled to play out. The way a person interacts with others, sets life goals, performs at work, his or her philosophy on life, and even his or her dress are written into this map.

The social status of one's parents, mental capabilities, physical characteristics and parental expectations are just a few of the ingredients which contribute to this special blueprint. The young boy who is shown love by his parents will develop this into his self-concept. If he is taught that he is of little value and not loved, he will develop a blueprint which reflects this. As this child builds a concept of who he is, his personal expectations are deeply ingrained. A life map is built upon a person's picture of himself or herself and the perception he or she believes others have of him or her.

The culture's social structure as well as the influence of parents and other individuals important to a child influences this development as well. This is clearly illustrated by the caste system in India. In that country, an infant is born into a caste or class of people. Regardless of his or her innate abilities or internal drive, he or she cannot move from a lower caste into a caste of greater affluence. At the time of the origin of our own country, certain social restrictions were imposed which limited the roles a person could assume in society. In order to be an elected official, for example, a person had to be white, male, a citizen of the United States, and a property owner. A black girl could not expect to someday become the President or hold any other elected office.

Family, friends, social status and self-concept are each characteristics which influence the life blueprint. Plainly stated, a blueprint of life is an inner message which directs both the immediate and long-term actions which a person takes.

People carry within themselves something like a portable tape recorder, which is always playing softly but insistently inside them. The message drawn into the tape is influenced even before they are born. The mother's emotions communicate the first sense of understanding that a child has about himself. When first born, the attitudes and communication that a child receives form lasting impressions. As the infant grows and matures, each experience builds upon others to form the life blueprint. It is as if people carry a picture of themselves around inside them that was created brush-stroke by brush-stroke by those who have touched their lives from the time they were small. Each brush adds a new dimension to the painting. The brush-strokes painted on the canvas early in life when it is bare and uncluttered are the strokes that are the most significant.

A life plan is based upon early influences and decisions made by the child. It is then built and reinforced by parents and events. The child's life map is generally 'set' prior to the age of six. For this reason, the Jesuits say, 'Give me a child for seven years and I care not who has him thereafter.' Proverbs 22:6 states, 'Train up a child in the way he should go: and when he is old, he will not depart from it' (KJV).

Foundational Qualities

The Lord has preordained the particular culture and sub-cultures into which each person is born (Psalm 139:16). The distinctive qualities of their influence helps to provide each person with a unique blueprint. The responsible believer will take advantage of the many qualities in his or her background and personality and develop them into a direction which will be pleasing unto the Lord.

Often, after responsible Christians examine their view of the world, their communication with others, their production at work, their social or economic status, or even their philosophy of life, they determine that they would like to change. Some characteristics, however, are deeply etched into their blueprint, and cannot easily be erased. In the section on values, we described these values as *primitive* and noted that they form the foundation for the person's total make-up. *Secondary* values are built upon the primitive values and can be adjusted more easily. For example, a person can change many of his behavior patterns (secondary) such as his gestures, vocabulary, attitude, and even his approach to people, without changing the innate qualities of his personality (primitive values).

Such change is well illustrated by the life of a successful church planter who was very shy as a boy. During the early years of his marriage, his fear of people led him to sit on the back row during church services. He quickly slipped out during the closing prayer to avoid having to speak with others. More than once, he and his wife returned to their car and drove home when they discovered a back row seat was not available.

Called to the ministry, he left his home community for Bible training. He recognized that his shyness was a tremendous handicap and approached his problem systematically. Increased exposure to new individuals and situations led to involvement in Sunday School, Vacation Bible Schools, and ultimately to becoming the lay pastor of a very small country church. After graduating from school, he was commissioned as a missionary. By continuing to expose himself to new people and increased opportunities to expand his *comfort zones* he became more assertive and outgoing. Through conscious effort he was able to overcome his handicap and was eventually instrumental in establishing a number of new churches, an expanding camping program, and an ongoing training program for his lay pastors. People who knew him before he left his home community could recognize his tremendous change in behavior (shyness), but his inner person (primitive quality) was still the same.

Self-image

Another quality which influences alterations in a blueprint of life is a person's self-image. One middle aged man, who had once been athletically inclined, noted that he weighed nearly 180 lbs. For his height, this was 35 lbs. more than he should have weighed. For some time, he viewed himself as an overweight person. With this image, he followed the life map of hearty eating. Try as he might, he had difficulty changing his habits and losing weight. He had to change the image he had of himself before he was able to make the behavioral change necessary to lose the required weight. A change in his self-image helped give him the discipline to change the part of his blueprint which related to eating habits and exercise. With a self perception that he was 'a skinny person in a fat body trying to get out,' he began a weight loss and exercise program. He eventually lost the pounds he had added over the years and was able to maintain his ideal weight.

Ill-Designed Blueprint

Sometimes the message that a person hears about himself or herself or other aspects of his or her life are not correct. This can create frustration and conflict. The maxim 'know thyself' can pay invaluable dividends. Even late in life, an inaccurate message can cause a person to play a role which is not congruent with his make-up. Students, for example, have been known to fail in school because of inaccurate beliefs about their abilities. Coach Darrel Mudra of Western Illinois University tells a story that portrays well this perspective. He explains that he had a student at Greeley who scored in the 98 percentile of the entrance test. The student thought that meant he had a 98 I.Q. Since he believed he was an average kid, he knew college would be hard for him. He almost failed in his first term. Between semesters he told his parents he did not believe he was college caliber. His parents took him back to school to talk with the college counselor. When he found out that 98 percentile score meant that he had a 140 I.Q. and was of superior intelligence his grades scored. Before the year was over he was doing 'A' work.

Redesigning the Blueprint

Redesigning a blueprint or a portion of it requires that a person recognize who he is, how he would like to be, and develop steps toward that end. In Luke 14:28, Jesus emphasized the importance of making realistic plans before acting. He stated, 'For which of you, intending to build a tower, sitteth not down first, and counteth the cost, whether he have sufficient to finish it?' (KJV)

The man who lost 35 lbs. recognized the way he looked and then pictured himself the way he would like to be. He designed a healthful diet and exercise plan and determined a specific date to begin this change. As a result of his action, he was able to change a portion of his life blueprint.

There are many examples in the scriptures of people who made changes in their life map. Moses' role as the leader of Israel necessitated a drastic change in image and behavior from that of a sheep herder to a ruler of men. Paul revised his role from that of aggressively stocking and persecuting others to gathering people to teach them love and forgiveness.

Amos was a fig picker. His social position was similar to a migrant fruit picker in today's American culture. He was not qualified scholastically or socially to speak with authority to the leaders of the day. Following God's instructions, he altered his programmed blueprint and made a mark in history.

Each Christian today should endeavor to gain a realistic understanding of his life map. He can then endeavor to establish realistic steps toward altering those parts which will help him to become a more effective servant of God.

ENVIRONMENT FOR GROWTH

If a child lives with criticism,
He learns to condemn.
If a child lives with hostility,
He learns to fight.
If a child lives with ridicule,
He learns to be shy.
If a child lives with shame,
He learns to feel guilty.

If a child lives with tolerance,
He learns to be patient.

If a child lives with encouragement,
He learns confidence.
If a child lives with praise,
He learns to appreciate.
If a child lives with fairness,
He learns justice.
If a child lives with security,
He learns to have faith.
If a child lives with approval,
He learns to like himself.
If a child lives with acceptance and friendship,
He learns to find life in the world.

Dorothy Law Nolte

The above poem cites the importance of a person's social environment. The child who is placed in a wholesome environment will develop healthy traits. A child in a poor environment will likewise reap unhealthy traits. In 1924, during the rise of behaviorist psychology, one of its advocates, Dr. John B. Watson, said, 'Give me a dozen healthy infants, well-formed, and my own special world to bring them up in, and I'll guarantee to take any one at random and train him to become any type of specialist I might select - doctor, lawyer, artist, merchant-chief, and yes, beggar and thief, regardless of his talents, tendencies, abilities, vocations, and race of his ancestors.'

Although Dr. Watson was more confident of the

importance of environment than today's psychologists, the significance of one's surroundings must not be neglected. In Proverbs 22:6, King Solomon says, 'Train up a child in the way he should go: and when he is old, he will not depart from it' (KJV). The importance of a child's environment has been proven in study after study. One such study concluded that children of parents with low IQ's will also generally have low IQ's. The exception was that children with parents depressed IQ's can do as well or even better than average if they are put in a favorable environment at an early age.

The Christian parent should be concerned about the type of environment which he allows for himself and his family. In Proverbs 13:20, King Solomon reveals the influence one's associates can assert. 'He that walketh with wise men shall be wise: but a companion of fools shall be destroyed' (KJV).

The Christian who spends his or her time with other believers who are excited about their church and all that is and can be accomplished is likely to be caught up in the concept of a progressive ministry. If he or she spends time with people who are discouraged with their church and who do not believe that much can be accomplished, he or she will likewise be influenced by their thinking. Christians, like everyone else, are influenced by those with whom they associate.

Dr. David C. McClelland described a study which substantiates this premise. He relates that in a Harvard study, a group of underachieving 14 year-olds were trained in achievement motivation. The boys who continued to improve after a two-year period were the middle-class boys. After careful study psychologists concluded that the lower-class boys dropped back because they returned to an environment in which neither parents nor friends encouraged achievement.

As responsible men and women of God believers are responsible for insuring that they allow themselves to be influenced by people and things which will strengthen them and their ministries in the eyes of God.

Blaming others for their situation, good or bad, is both popular and convenient for many people. They consider themselves victims of their environment and feel there is nothing they can do to alter their situation. While it is true that people are a product of their past influences, it is also true that they are responsible to God for the way they react to unavoidable situations. Moreover, they are also responsible for many of the positions that they allow themselves to be in.

Unjustly thrown into prison, Joseph demonstrated maturity and leadership. Consequently, he was placed in charge of prison operations (Genesis 39:21-23). The Apostle Paul, when thrown into jail, accepted his situation and learned to make the most of it. In I Thessalonians 5:18, he writes, 'In everything give thanks: for this is the will of God in Christ Jesus concerning you.' (KJV)

These men were not able to *control* their surroundings, but they were able to adjust their attitudes toward these surroundings so that the experience *added to* their character development instead of defeating them.

A parishioner stated to her pastor that she had given up on waiting for her 'ship to come in'. She said she believed that it had been 'torpedoed and sunk'. This lady lost the belief that she had control over her environment in any way and instead felt like a victim of circumstances.

Christians owe it to themselves, their families and to God to take charge of as many of the influences in their surroundings as they can. Christianity is based upon the concept that, 'If any man be in Christ, he is a new creation:

old things are passed away; behold, all things are become new' (II Corinthians 5:17). If a spiritual newness is possible, then the life which it affects should reflect this. Christians should not blame their parents, past experience, the world, or anything else. Forgetting the past, they should place themselves in a position to fulfill God's call for them to the best of their ability. William H. Cook has stated:

If you feed your faith, your faith will grow.
If you feed your doubts, your doubts will grow.
Whichever one you feed will surely grow.

In Philippians 3:13-14, Paul speaks of placing his past behind him and pressing on 'toward the high calling of God'. Today's believers should put aside past experiences and start afresh, exposing themselves to environments which will enhance their spiritual well-being and effectiveness as children and servants of God.

ATTITUDE FOR GROWTH

'For as he thinketh in his heart, so is he.'
Proverbs 23:7 (KJV)

The person who takes a pro-active perspective toward life will set the tone for the attitude of those around him. If he is creative, congenial, organized, visionary and hard working the people around him will be infected by his attitude. The general spirit of those who come into contact with him will be influenced in a positive way.

Christian men and women should recognize that they have the power to influence the attitude of the people with whom they work. A 'Can Do' attitude can make the difference between whether a business will fail or succeed or whether a family will grow together through a crisis or dissolve.

The pastors in two neighboring communities had the responsibility for churches of similar size. One pastor was vitally concerned with the spiritual and personal growth of each person in the community. As this attitude of concern was exemplified, it was reflected by the people in the church. Many new programs were instituted to reach the needs of the people in the community. This growing ministry acquired a reputation of being a 'friendly' place to worship.

The second pastor showed a sense of pessimism. He feared that the ministry would fail. He had a poor attitude toward others and pointed out their personal and family problems. He cited the need for others to change and start new programs but demonstrated little benevolence or skill in helping them work things out. His church developed a poor reputation in the community and experienced neither spiritual nor numerical growth.

An attitude toward life is a reflection of the inner person. Three thousand years ago King Solomon wrote, 'For as he thinketh in his heart, so is he' (Proverbs 23:7 - KJV). A Christian may feel, for example, that he or she is governed by Murphy's Law, which states that if anything can go wrong, it will. With a base of operation like this, his or her actions will no doubt conform to this personal philosophy. The spiritual leader who lives by the rule, 'This is the day which the LORD hath made; we will rejoice and be glad in it' (Psalm 118:24 - KJV) will have a much different base from which to work. The missionary with an optimistic 'Can Do' view of the world will see things differently than one who is ruled by Murphy's Law.

The implications of a healthy attitude are expressed in a story carried many years ago in the *Sunday School Times*.

'One day a mover's wagon came past Farmer Jones's gate. Farmer Jones was friendly to everybody, so he asked the mover where they were going.

"We are moving from Johnstown to Jamestown," they told him. "Can you tell us what kind of neighbors we will find there?"

"What kind did you find in Johnstown?"

"The very worst kind," they said, "gossipy, unkind, and indifferent. We were glad to move away."

"You will find the same in Jamestown."

The next day another mover's wagon passed, and a similar conversation took place. The second party asked what neighbors they would find in Johnstown and were asked the kind they had found in Jamestown.

"The very best, so kind and considerate, it almost broke our hearts to move away."

"You will find exactly the same kind in Johnstown," was the farmer's reply.'

As parents, spouses, neighbors, community leaders and members of the Parent Teacher Association, Christian men and women are responsible for more than just themselves. They are also held accountable for the influence which they have upon others. They should have a healthy attitude toward

God, man and the world in general. Their example and instruction will be reflected in the lives of others.

Every person experiences disappointments and hurts. The response to these setbacks will determine their influence on one's life. If bitterness, aggression or withdrawal are the reaction, they will prove to be a destructive influence. If they are met with the attitude that these situations are opportunities for personal and spiritual growth, their influence will be just that. James 1:2-4 states:

> *'Consider it pure joy, my brothers, whenever you face trials of many kinds, because you know that the testing of your faith develops perseverance. Perseverance must finish its work so that you may be mature and complete, not lacking anything.' (NIV)*

The perception of any event is all-important. Psalm 118:24 is not rhetoric; it is the foundation for a healthy attitude and view of the world.

It has been stated that the way a person reacts to the storms of life can be equated to a pebble in a mountain stream. As torrents of water come pounding down upon it, it will either become smooth and polished or it will break and be destroyed. A responsible child of God will endeavor to approach each situation with the attitude that it will bring him or her greater personal maturity and growth in Christ, smoothing and polishing his or her character. II Corinthians 4:8,9 states: 'We are troubled on every side, yet not distressed; we are perplexed, but not in despair; persecuted, but not forsaken; cast down, but not destroyed' (KJV).

A mature and responsible child of God recognizes that he must be responsible for his perception of the world. The irresponsible person will feel victimized and caught in an emotional state over which he has no control. Of all of God's creation man alone can change his own destiny by simply altering his perception of the world.

While attending college, I worked for several years as a hospital orderly. Late one winter, a young woman who had previously attended my church was admitted. Deathly ill, she complained of abdominal pains of an 'undefined origin'. Soon she was moved into the Intensive Care Unit where she was carefully monitored. She became progressively more despondent until she appeared totally incoherent. The doctor could not find any physical symptoms which would give him a clue as to the root of her distress. As she became weaker, death seemed imminent. As a last resort, the doctor marched into her room and scolded her. He demanded that she 'straighten up and think of others; not just of herself'. To the nurse's surprise, the patient responded to the scolding. With the guidance of a psychiatrist and the hospital chaplain, she quickly recovered, returning home two weeks later. This story is the exception, but it illustrates the extent to which a responsible attitude can affect a person's life.

A Christian should learn to accept his or her environment and pressures, relying upon the Lord to help him or her work through the difficulties with which he or she is confronted. Romans 8:28 states, 'And we know that all things work together for good to them that love God, to them who are the called according to his purpose' (KJV).

A mature attitude is very important to a healthy mental outlook. People who demonstrate pessimism about themselves, their ministries and life in general will not experience the same ministry effectiveness as those who strive to gain an optimistic, yet realistic view. The grumblers, faultfinders and rationalizers are not the doers in life. Men and women who build happy, balanced lives are those who realize the potential which exists in any situation.

A seminary student, for example, was called to a small church located in a remote area some distance from the seminary. The old building which existed had not been used for several years and it showed evidence of severe neglect. The ministry had been closed due to a heated dispute which split the church and rocked the community. The newly-opened church presented many challenges. Realizing the difficulties which lay ahead, the layman firmly believed he could have an effective ministry. With a belief in the mission which God had sent him to do, he demonstrated a vision for the community and love for its people. As the years progressed, the mission point grew into a thriving church. A new building was built and a parsonage secured. A lesser man would have looked at the initial situation and turned away. However, with a sense of optimism, vision for the community and willingness to work, this man demonstrated what a healthy and God-honoring attitude could accomplish.

Everyone is ultimately responsible for their thoughts and actions. The attitudes of bitterness and peace, optimism and pessimism, happiness and soberness, melancholy and concern are controlled by the individual. As Norman Wright keenly noted, 'Two men looked out from prison bars, One saw mud, one saw stars.'

Every aspect of a Christian's life is influenced by his or her frame of reference. Christian men and women must therefore strive to understand themselves and those things which affect their outlooks on life. They can then endeavor to control their attitudes and the situations which influence these attitudes. The result should bring glory to God through greater ministry effectiveness, increased family harmony, and sincere concern for others.

FLEXIBILITY FOR GROWTH

Hanging on a wall in Buckingham Palace is a framed copy of a simple prayer. It reads, 'Teach me to cry neither for the moon nor over spilt milk.' King George V hung these words as a reminder that some things can be changed and others cannot. A healthy person will learn which things he can alter and which things he must adjust to.

Change is an inevitable part of everyone's life. Children are born into a family, grow up, and leave; friends change jobs and move away; society changes in the wave of new technological advances. Flexibility and the ability to adjust ourselves are often the key for survival in our fast-paced world.

In 1980 NEXT magazine displayed the following words in an ad for their periodical:

Just for fun, can you guess what do the following things all have in common - -

Pocket Calculators	*Hot Tubs*	*Gay Lib*
Women's Lib	*Plains, Ga*	*Mopeds*
OPEC	*TM*	*Cholesterol Scare*
Legionnaire's Disease	*EST*	*Swine Flu Scare*
Deep Throat	*PCB*	*Saccharin Scare*
Moonies	*ERA*	*Asbestos Scare*

*The answer - ten years ago you had **never heard** of any of them! What will the coming decade bring forth? Heaven only knows.*

Since the writing of this ad, many new technological advances and sociological changes have taken place, and we have little control over many of them. Some represent tremendous improvements to the world, western society, the Christian community, and today's families, but many do not. The key to a healthy mental attitude is to discover which things can be changed, which things cannot be changed, which things are worth fighting for, and which things necessitate flexibility.

Reinhold Niebuhr wrote a short prayer which has gained notable popularity. It accurately describes the underlying philosophy concerning healthy flexibility. It reads, 'God, give me the serenity to accept what cannot be changed, the courage to change what should be changed, and the wisdom to distinguish the one from the other.'

The person who wishes to live a full and healthy life must learn what can be, should be, and cannot be changed.

Dogmatism

Flexibility is a master key that opens the door of opportunity. Dogmatism on the other hand locks the door of new insights and increased understanding. Dogmatism is a dictatorial, steadfast assertion of an opinion or belief. The dogmatic person is 'close-minded'. He has already made up his mind and doesn't want to be confused by facts or logic.

Dogmatism should not of course be confused with foundational beliefs. Many beliefs, especially those biblical or moral in nature, are fundamental and should not be compromised. The doctrinal statement of a church, for example, holds the truths which the congregation feels cannot be compromised. In the same way, each person who knows who he is as a person understands many of the beliefs which form his own moral standards. These standards are important and should remain steadfast. They create the base from which to make decisions and develop further character.

Aside from these foundational beliefs, a person should be open to the ideas and concepts of others. A mature person should show good judgment in knowing when to be open to the suggestions, ideas and interpretations of others and when to stand fast defending fundamental principles.

Knowing when and how to change and accept New Ideas
Some degree of change is evidenced in each person's life, but it should not serve as a means of escape from difficult circumstances. The age-old saying that 'the grass is greener on the other side of the fence' may seem true, but even though things may *seem* better elsewhere, they may not always *be* better. A manager of a small East Coast firm, for example, became caught up in the mosaic of difficult situations inherent in any business. Differences of personalities, varied priorities, financial limitations, and slow but steady progress plagued him. Others outside his position could see the tremendous and unique potential of his position. Some eyed his work almost with envy. But this ambitious manager looked only at the daily trials, set-backs and disappointments. Like many rising stars in the business world he was offered a position in a nearby city. He leaped for the position, seeing it as 'a way out' of his present situation. Several years later in a letter to his friends at the Home Office of the original firm he revealed that he was once again in a similar situation. Although the people and location were different, the types and degrees of programs remained relatively the same. His old position progressed in its prescribed course and someone else was reaping the reward of his efforts. He had learned that

change does not always result in a better situation. If it is a means for running away from something, it may prove to be more of a defeat than a blessing. The story of the prodigal son (Luke 15:11-32) is a good example of someone who found that running away would not solve his problem. It is through inner growth that personal strength and peace develop. The fable that things are better elsewhere is well-illustrated in a poem by Theodosia Garrison:

The Gypsies passed her little gate,
She stopped her wheel to see;
A brown-faced pair who walked the road
Free as the wind is free.
And suddenly her tidy room
A prison seemed to be.

Her shiny plates against the walls,
Her sunlit, sanded floor,
The brass-bound wedding chest that held
Her linens' snowy store,
The very wheel whose humming died—
Seemed only chains she bore.

She watched two foot-free Gypsies pass,
She never knew or guessed
The wistful dream that held them close,
The longing in each breast—
Some day to know a home like hers
Wherein their hearts might rest.

The Difficulty in Change
Significant or abrupt change is difficult. Gradual change, at least to some degree, is an innate part of everyone's life and

is not always noticeable. A distinct act which represents a move from the known to the unknown is not easy; even obvious change which may seem natural and healthy to others may create tremendous anxiety.

Viktor Frankl writes in his book *Man's Search for Meaning* about his fellow prisoners in the Nazi concentration camp at Dachau. Some of the prisoners, who yearned desperately for their freedom, had been held captive for many years. When they were eventually released, they walked out into the sunlight, blinked nervously and then silently walked back into the familiar darkness of the prisons, to which they had been accustomed for such a long time.

Significant change is difficult because most people crave stability. Stability provides assurance of personal identity and relationships with others. The person who comes from a stable environment knows others' expectations of him, his social role, and his value to others. New surroundings and relationships create a need to re-establish stability in each of these areas.

In this sense, habits can be a healthful and productive part of life. According to the dictionary, *habit* is a tendency or disposition to act in a certain way, acquired by repetition of such acts. Without habits, man would be forced to think about everything he did. He would need to be aware of each stroke of his toothbrush, each chew of food, and the angle of the foot for each step taken. For example, when playing basketball a fine athlete will not take conscious thought of each bounce of the ball. By habit, the ball is dribbled so that concentration can be placed upon where to run, to whom to pass, or from which angle to shoot. Habit can be very helpful.

While habits are essential for survival, they can also deter progress. Habits create an atmosphere of comfort, so departure from the normal routine, exposure to new people, or an encounter with a new environment will create the need to develop new actions and habits. The process of discovering what these new routines should be requires confronting the unknown which naturally creates fear. The degree varies between people and situations, but fear of the unknown is natural. One authority colorfully likens it to stepping from one rock to the next while crossing a mountain stream. While resting on any one rock there is a sense of security and safety. There is of course no movement, progress or satisfaction beyond safety. The challenge is to step to the next rock. This movement is frightening because of the short moment when a person is not firmly rooted on neither rock.

Change can be frightening and difficult. It often takes several months or years for a person to become settled into a new job, marriage or city. This is particularly difficult for young professionals graduating from college and entering the work force in a new city. Moving to a new area results in exposure to new customs, a different type of work, and a changed mode of relationships. As they become acquainted with new surroundings, some aspects may make them question their abilities and competency in making the necessary transition to the new demands on them. In college, they served under the supervision of the school administration and faculty. As a professional, the quality and quantity of work, style of leadership, and methods used are often left to them. No longer a student consumed with learning, they are now producing. Things which once had little meaning such as the style of dress and personal habits are now carefully scrutinized and become very important.

Such a change requires new types of relationships and roles in life. Depending upon the personality of the person and the intensity of the pressure of the position, the difficulty of change will vary. For some it will seem natural, for others it will not.

A change in role may alter how the person perceives himself or herself. The director of a youth camp, for example, experienced a theft problem at one of his camps. Valuable items were found missing from a number of cabins. Once the thief was caught, the camp director decided to handle the child, not as a criminal but as a lonely child who needed to feel special. Commissioned as the director's personal helper, the child made a complete about-face in conduct and attitude. He no longer considered himself a bad boy. Instead, he was a camp leader. In order to be a camp leader, a person had to be good. His image of himself changed, resulting in a modification of his actions and personal identity.

Change will result in the creation of new roles, responsibilities, and relationships. Fear of the unknown and the value of these changes can cause a person to hesitate at the slightest thought of change. For a church congregation the addition of a worship service, a change in Sunday School curriculum, or even adding new songs to the order of worship can cause such fear. For the pastor, this can be frustrating. These frustrations can be minimized if he realizes the root of resistance to change and takes steps to help ease the fear. Gradual change over an extended period of time may ease the trauma.

People will find that over time they develop a habit with which they are comfortable for dealing with most aspects of his or her life. A break in routine or the introduction of new or assertive personalities into his or her life may threaten their role and the actions that they take. This may create anxiety. Change in environment or role will affect their habits, actions and relationships. With this change will come the need to adjust. Such an alteration may be frightening and not welcomed, since they are comfortable with the status quo instead.

The thrust of this book is change. People need to be willing to examine each area of their life and determine whether change is needed. If they are not completely satisfied that they have developed their talents in proportion to what God would have, they should take steps to more fully utilize the potential with which God has endowed them.

Successful change necessitates the presence of a strong, inner (intrinsic) desire for progress. Many people have resolved to lose weight, but have found it to be a difficult task. One young father who lost nearly 40 pounds contributes his loss to an innate decision to make whatever changes were needed to reach his goal. Although others encouraged him, only he could make the decision. Once he determined that his weight was a significant priority, he altered much of his life. He changed his eating and exercise habits, the type of food and frequency of eating took a new shape and his daily work and social schedule took on new dimensions. After a few months, his self-image took a sharp jump. The courage and discipline involved in taking these actions resulted in a new level of self-confidence; enough to change jobs, beginning an exciting and rewarding career.

Change requires wisdom to know what to alter, and what to leave the same. It necessitates risk and involves the fear of the unknown. Without change, a person cannot develop his innate talents and abilities. Healthful change requires a basic plan and understanding of what is to be accomplished along the way. Time is required for natural, systematic development. The person who wishes to become all that he can be for Christ should prayerfully identify the need for change, accept the possibility of what can be done, develop a systematic plan of action, and be willing to work toward the end that he has decided upon.

VISION FOR GROWTH

'The Dreamers of the day are dangerous people, for they may act their dreams with open eyes to make them possible.'

T. E. Lawrence

Vision does not need to be confined to the dreamer of dreams. To the contrary, the innovators and 'doers' in today's world must be able to envision the many possibilities which exist within their lives. People who have a vision for their lives will know what they would like to do and this can determine what actually can be accomplished. Practical steps can then be designed to make the vision a reality.

The Apostle Paul is a fine example of a man of God who not only had a desire to reach lost souls for Christ, but also had a vision of how this might be accomplished. In Romans 15:28, Paul shares his plan for a missionary trip to Spain. He envisioned spreading the gospel throughout the civilized world. Without a vision, he would not have travelled to distant cities, establishing congregations at key points of his journey.

Several characteristics which Paul possessed are essential if a person is to see a dream effectively become a reality. First, Paul placed his confidence in Christ. He believed that the projects which he undertook were *in accordance with God's will* for his life. He had no doubt that the course of his action had the support of his Lord.

Second, Paul was willing to *work*. Tenacity, hard work and discipline each took their place in translating his vision into reality. The weariness of long and dangerous travel, confrontations with skilled theologians and the necessity to work to pay his way necessitated a willingness to work hard through difficult circumstances.

Third, Paul looked to Christ both for the *strength* and for the wisdom and endurance to see his dream fulfilled. With Christ as his guide, he was not afraid to 'press toward the mark' (Philippians 3:14 - KJV). He believed that what he was doing was for Christ and could be accomplished through Christ. His motivation was not centered upon himself, but upon his usefulness as a servant of his King.

The significance of these three factors is evidenced by examining the cases of two ministers, Alan and Brian. Both men graduated from the same school, had similar family situations and their natural abilities were comparable.

Alan was very conscious of the growth in the number of people involved in his ministry. During professional conferences, he frequently participated in the futile exercise of comparing numbers, growth patterns and programs with other ministers. Even though Alan felt a definite call to the ministry, he did not feel burdened for the people with whom he worked. Long on goals, Alan neglected to complement these goals with the hard work and discipline needed to make them a reality. He arose late in the morning and was not perceived as particularly productive or disciplined by his constituency. In addition, Alan did not spend a great deal of time studying the scriptures. He once commented that he was just not disciplined enough to have a daily devotional time. It appeared that Alan placed little reliance upon the Lord for strength. After only several years of service, Alan left the pastorate, amidst feelings of doubt and discouragement.

His colleague, Brian, was subtly different. First, he felt a definite call, not only to the ministry in general, but also to the people on his field. His written goals for the ministry reflected a concern for their spiritual maturity as well as an increase in church attendance. He showed keen concern for people as individuals. Second, Brian was not afraid of work. Although he was careful not to neglect his family, he started his day early and developed a course of action for work to be performed as he carefully scheduled his week. Long hours and the development of new programs specifically geared to reach his people created an intrinsic satisfaction which tended to drive him on. Third, Brian daily committed his work to God. His ministry was not motivated by the need for notoriety. Instead, his concern was to spread the message of Christ. Because of the need he saw in the lives of others, he relied heavily upon the strength and guidance of God to direct the scope and intensity of his outreach. Over the course of his fruitful ministry, Brian was responsible for the implementation of many programs and the spiritual growth of many people.

Vision is a necessary element of any person who wishes to live a full and productive life. The effect of Paul's vision upon his ministry demonstrates its importance. He had a definite call and a passion to fulfill his assignment. His vision grew and blossomed because it was supported by a sound structure. The Apostle Paul had a definite call; he was disciplined and not afraid of hard work, and he relied upon God for wisdom and strength. Had Paul failed to have a sound base for his vision, he, like Alan, may have diminished the effectiveness of his service.

The Need

Every area of one's life carries with it the need for varied degrees of vision. A person's dreams concerning his or her marital relationship, family life, hobbies, spiritual maturity, development of talents and skills require vision. The couple who wish to start a family envision the number of children they would like to have, the way in which they would like to raise them, and special events in their lives. They dream of teaching their children to walk, ride a bicycle, and drive a car. The standards and expectations which they have for their child's achievements and activities are parts of the vision process. Without envisioning the future, people will approach it randomly. Ephesians 5:15,16 warns the believer to be 'very careful, then, how you live - not as unwise but as wise, making the most of every opportunity, because the days are evil' (NIV).

Any responsible Christian should look into the future, envisioning and analyzing the possibilities which exist for him or her and those who are influenced by him or her.

The Scope

The scope of these dreams should include each area of life considered to be significant. The goals established by such vision should be realistic, wholesome and compatible with other dreams, obligations and one's relationship with God. The book of Proverbs adeptly states healthy guidelines for goals:

'Remove far from me vanity and lies: give me neither
poverty nor riches; feed me with food convenient for
me: Lest I be full, and deny thee, and say, Who is the
LORD? or lest I be poor, and steal, and take the name
of my God in vain.'   (Proverbs 30:8-9 - KJV)

A healthy vision is congruent with other dreams and
obligations. It also supports spiritual maturity.

While it is true that no man knows the future (James 4:13-
17), it is also true that each one 'who knows the good he ought
to do and doesn't do it, sins' (James 4:17 - NIV). In this light,
the believer should gain a view of what he feels God would
have him do. He can then become sensitive to the direction
of the Holy Spirit as he undertakes the process of making his
vision a reality. Paul demonstrated such sensitivity in Acts
16:7, 'When they came to the border of Mysia, they tried to
enter Bithynia, but the Spirit of Jesus would not allow them
to' (NIV). Paul altered his vision based upon his keen
sensitivity to the Holy Spirit.

A second career minister came to the pastorate after early
retirement from another career. As a dedicated family man,
he had envisioned raising his family and maintaining an
active stance in his local church. His vision changed when
he felt led by God to attend Bible College and acquired the
credentials needed to move into Christian service. Today, as
an active minister, his life is evidence that vision can change
in a spiritually beneficial way when the Christian remains in
tune to the leading of the Holy Spirit.

More often than not, a person will envision future
development within safer boundaries than are really
necessary. According to Richard Bolles, a national leader in
career development, for every person who *over-dreams* of

doing more than they are able, there are four people who *under-dream*. They sell themselves short.

A person needs to be careful when planning for future developments to dream dreams which are high enough to be challenging and to insure proper development of the resources God has entrusted to them. They should also be low enough to be realistically achieved.

People are dynamic, that is, they are constantly changing. If they do not grow, stagnation quickly sets and they begin to decline. Without dreams and goals toward which to strive, life loses excitement and becomes dull and boring. This is graphically seen in men and women who retire. Those who remain active typically remain in good health and live long, happy lives. Retirees who sit back and smell the roses dry up and die.

Carl Bates described the impact that adequate vision can have on a person's life and ministry. He recalled the realization and insight that he received about vision and goal setting. He stated that there came a time in his life in which he earnestly prayed: 'God, I want Your power!' but nothing seemed to change. One day feeling the deep burden for more strength to carry out his ministry he prayed, 'God, why haven't You answered that prayer?' To him it seemed as if God quietly whispered back the simple reply, 'With plans no bigger than yours, you don't need My power.'

Without vision, the Christian man or woman will accomplish little. It is when a person has a dream that he or she is forced to stretch himself or herself and develop the inner qualities which God has provided.

The Fear of Failure
Many people are fearful of aiming too high because they fear

the taste of failure. The thought of humiliation, and loss of respect by others and themselves, intimidates them. This makes it difficult for them to strike out on their own and try to accomplish anything which is not safe, guaranteed success.

A very successful church planter explains that not every Sunday School, Bible study or church which he tried to start emerged into the final form which he envisioned. Some were abandoned before they were started, others were discontinued after a short period of time, and some grew rapidly. The greatest reward lay in those that grew to a level of maturity and maintained a vibrant witness to their community. Along the way there were setbacks and discouragements. According to him, 'The one who has never failed at anything is the one who hasn't tried anything.'

Dreams serve as the catalyst which stretch a person to develop beyond his current state. The Apostle Paul dreamed of undertaking several missionary journeys. As he pursued each one, he encountered many setbacks and discouragements. A lesser man would have allowed the intimidations of skillful Jewish scholars or the humiliation of public scourging to defeat him, but Paul had a vision. It was due to these pictured goals that he endured the setbacks and apparent failures of the present. Even after publicly announcing his dreams, Paul sometimes failed to reach his goal. In Romans 15:28, Paul shares his desire to travel to Spain. Records are unavailable to substantiate such a journey, but Paul is not considered to be a failure. To the contrary, he was willing to envision goals and work toward their completion, ('making the most of every opportunity' - Ephesians 5:16 - NIV) and was responsible for spreading the gospel throughout much of the (what was then) known world.

Christian men and women owe it to themselves, their

children, spouse, employer, church and God to envision of healthy growth in each area of life. Not only will they benefit personally but so will those who are around them.

Dr. William H. Cook shares an experience which depicts the importance of properly balanced vision. He states that while leading conferences for pastors in India he heard one of the pastors share a startling opinion of American Christians. He stated, 'You know what the problem with American Christians is? They think so small. Imagine someone being a small thinker in the world's biggest business!'

The person who is the true failure is one who has a narrow vision or one who has no vision at all.

The Acceptance of Natural Limits

Properly balanced dreams demand that natural, rational limitations be recognized. Verses such as Matthew 15:28, 17:20, 21:22, and Mark 9:23 and 11:24 support the concept that 'I can do all things through Christ which strengtheneth me' (Philippians 4:13 - KJV). These statements lie within certain contexts. First, they necessitate a reliance upon the Lord. Second, 'I can' requires logical credible thinking. People cannot grow wings or physically be in Philadelphia and Portland at the same time. Common sense and good judgment must accompany the principle of visionary thinking. Each person has certain natural limitations, which may be imposed by genetic or temperamental factors, or formative environmental events, but each person excels in some other areas. Honest integrity demands that a person admit there are some things he or she cannot do, some battles they cannot win and some goals they cannot achieve.

The Apostle Paul, for example, prayed that his infirmities

would be taken from him, but God chose that his affliction
should remain with him. If Paul had chosen to be discouraged
and angry with his situation, his ministry would have been
impaired. As it was, he accepted the Lord's will. No doubt
his 'affliction' was related to his eyesight. It was, therefore,
necessary for him to employ the aid of others in writing
epistles and to rely heavily upon God for the strength to do
many of the otherwise mundane things in life. Paul's attitude
of acceptance is reflected in a statement by Sir Philip
Snowden:

> *'This has been my philosophy of life. Try to shape*
> *circumstances; but when circumstances are too*
> *strong to be altered, then accept them with*
> *resignation and shape your actions and your*
> *conduct according to unalterable fate.'*

Such acceptance is not to preclude a balanced vision of the
future. Every person will find setbacks in his or her family
and profession. Nobel Prize winner William Shockly,
inventor of the transistor, said, 'When life gives you lemons,
make lemonade.' In a sense, this reflects the actions of Paul.
Restrained by the authorities while awaiting trial, Paul used
his exposure to his guards to share the message of Christ with
them. Paul had been given a 'lemon' but he chose to make
'lemonade' from it. Paul had learned what he could change
or alter and what to accept. Today's men and women of God
need to embark upon realistic visions which will stretch them
enough to allow growth, but which are realistic enough to be
feasible.

One young couple, for example, had a child with a
learning disability. Concerned for the child's welfare, the

parents contacted a number of physicians to determine what could be done to help the child live a full and normal life. A special diet, medication and a special education program were prescribed. With great care, the couple strictly carried out the instructions of their medical doctors. This couple accepted their situation as irrevocable. They then adjusted their dreams to adhere to the reality of the situation. Working closely with their child, they grew close as a family, setting their dreams on a much different level than if their child were not limited. The closeness which occurred and the steady progress of their child proved to be the 'lemonade'. They were able to look beyond the immediate difficulties which faced them and look to the future, envisioning what could and would be done for their child.

The Need for Hard Work
One ingredient which is contained in both the illustration of Paul and this young couple is the willingness to work as described earlier. Tenacity, diligence and discipline are each words which stand out as necessary if a vision is to become a reality. A dear friend, for example, is know by my colleagues as 'the' man of vision. Full of youthful ambition, he can sit by the hour and perpetuate ideas about ministry development and expansion. In his own ministry he has developed tremendous plans, carefully plotted out and realistic in nature. Unfortunately, he lacks the discipline and tenacity inherent to hard work. Because of this deficiency, his ministries have been short-lived, bearing little fruit.

As a young adult I carefully studied the characteristics of my father, a missionary with tremendous success in church planting and recruiting men to the ministry. I wanted to know the personal traits which led to his success. After careful study I concluded that the traits which contributed to his success were godliness, vision, enthusiasm, the gift of encouragement and hard work, which included discipline and tenacity.

Each person has areas within his or her life which he or she knows could be improved. Family relationships, listening skills, management of time, organization and spiritual depth each represent possible areas of need. People also have the ability to improve in these areas. A vision is necessary so he or she will know where to improve. He or she must also be willing to work diligently toward that end. Almost everything which a person does not like about himself is within his capacity to change if he will make the decision to do so. The decision must be followed up with hard work, but the point is that the choice is totally his.

Woodrow Wilson put it this way, 'All big men are dreamers. They see things in the soft haze of a spring day or in the red fire of a long winter's evening. Some of us let these great dreams die, but others nourish and protect them, nurse them through bad days 'til they bring them to the sunshine and light which comes always to those who sincerely hope that their dreams will come true.'

As children of God, Christian men and women should be willing to step back and look at each area of their lives. They can then depict how they would like to direct the development of each aspect during the coming years. By gaining a vision for the future and a willingness to work diligently toward that end, they can increase the fruitfulness of their lives and service, 'making the most of every opportunity, because the days are evil' (Ephesians 5:16 - NIV).

DIRECTION FOR GROWTH

The great thing in this world is not so much where
we are, but in what direction we are moving.
                                        Oliver Wendell Holmes

The scriptures point to the responsibility that each person has for his gifts: 'Neglect not the gift that is in thee' (I Timothy 4:14 - KJV). Again in I Peter 4:10 we find 'Each one should use whatever [spiritual] gift he has received to serve others' (NIV). I Corinthians 14:40 reminds us that 'everything should be done in a fitting and orderly way' (NIV), while remaining in tune with the Holy Spirit (Acts 16:7). Personal development, therefore, is required by God and should be carried out in 'a fitting and orderly way'.

Inherent to such a growth plan is the need for goals and objectives. The direction of these goals will determine which personal qualities are developed and to what extent they are developed. For example, some women consciously established as their life objective the role of a homemaker and helper to their husband. They concentrated their time on learning skills in sewing, child rearing, and teaching children's classes. Other women chose to have a career outside the home. They focus their energies on additional schooling and other professional training as well as on developing healthy family relationships. Both type of women know the direction they would like for their life to head and, therefore, are able to establish goals which supported her objectives.

Unfortunately, most people do not have specific written goals for their lives. As a result, they do not concentrate on developing in any one direction. This 'wandering effect' promotes very little expertise or experience.

Goal statements such as 'to bring glory to God' or 'to share Christ with others' sound very noble, but are nebulous rather than specific. Goals should be able to be measured by time (when it will be completed) and by action (what will be accomplished). They can then establish a specific direction so that plans for development can be built upon them. The person who has not determined at least to some degree the direction for his life, will not know on which areas to concentrate his development.

This direction provides more than just an understanding of how to create an effective personal growth profile. It also provides a zest for life and an inner motivation to achieve. Dr. John Haggai, noted lecturer and author, describes one of the most bitter and cynical men he has ever known as a man with tremendous talent. According to Dr. Haggai this man had more ability than most six men. He was an outstanding cartoonist, a top notch photographer, a gifted speaker, an outstanding writer and had superior skill in sales and administration. He has seen men who did not have a small fraction of this man's ability soar to the heights of success while he accomplished little with his life. The people who knew him knew the reason. He never came to the point at which he determined what he was going to do with his life. He was afraid to throw all his energies in a single project. Since he aimed at nothing, he had no target, making achievements impossible. He did not say with Paul the Apostle, 'this one thing I do.'

Men and women who wish a full and productive life must establish realistic goals for the major areas of their lives. Then they will be able to control effectively the development and direction of the qualities God has given to them.

General Goal Setting

A successful executive while just beginning his career took a close look at his life. He did this after hearing of an interesting survey taken of the students graduating from Harvard University's College of Business. In 1953 the students of the graduating class were asked whether or not they had established written goals for their lives. Of all the seniors only 3% had done so. Twenty years later in 1973 a survey of this same class was taken. It was found that the 3% who had written goals had been more productive, contributed more for the betterment of mankind and made more money than the other 97% combined. This study left a strong impression on the young man. He desired to be a responsible servant of God. Reviewing his attributes and liabilities, life dreams and current circumstances, he determined to establish realistic workable 'goals' or 'statements of intent' for his life.

Following a logical order, he commenced to divide his life into six major areas. These included 1) spiritual, 2) physical, 3) mental, 4) family/social, 5) career and 6) material sections. Having made these divisions, he contemplated each one. Prayerfully, he considered both immediate and long term options, weighing each one carefully. Writing down his thoughts about each area, he was soon able to bring order to his thoughts.

With care, he constructed a general purpose statement for each area of his life. The reason for this statement was to provide a general direction for each area. He weighed his thoughts, abilities, convictions and future intentions as they applied to each area. He then carefully drafted his purpose statement.

Having completed the purpose statement, he commenced to write five-year goals. This exercise required a great deal of time and effort. Restfully relaxing in a place of solitude, he imagined what he would like his life to be like five years from then. His imagination journeyed into his future, examining his home, family, job, friends and personal growth. With a pen at his side he was able to take notes of the things he saw and heard. Based upon his dreams, he set realistic five-year goals which he felt would help him realize his dream.

Not everyone can so easily establish long term objectives. For some, several weeks of contemplation might be necessary; even then, only moderately long term goals can then be established. Questions such as, 'If I knew that I were to die in six months, how would I live?' or 'At the end of my life, what do I want my eulogy to say?' might be helpful to stimulate thought. One gentleman took several consecutive evenings and made a list of the things he would ultimately like to have as a part of his life. He then prioritized this list and established time schedules for them. As a result, he had a general idea of what he would like to accomplish with his life and a reasonable guideline for establishing long term goals. One-year goals were established next. Each of these one-year goals supported the general purpose statement and the long term goals. So that he would be able to tell when or if he reached his goals, he wrote them so that they could be measured by both *time* and by action. The purpose statement and one-year goals for the physical aspect of the young man's life looked something like this:

PURPOSE STATEMENT: To be physically healthy to such an extent that I will have an alert mind, healthy self-image, and low susceptibility to disease.

ONE-YEAR GOALS:

1.   Establish and maintain a physical weight of 160 pounds or less between June 1, 19__ and January 1, 19__.

2.   Perform exercises, including a minimum of 100 push-ups, 100 sit-ups, 100 leg lifts, and 50 touch toes at least 4 times per week between March 3, 19__ and January 1, 19__.

Under the goal he listed specific steps which needed to be taken in order to accomplish the goal. These were divided into those things which needed immediate action and those which could be accomplished sometime in the future. Under weight loss, for example, he wrote the following steps:

IMMEDIATE STEPS LEADING TO THE GOAL:

1.   Observe daily weight fluctuation.

2.   Substitute sweets and breads with diet foods.

3.   Reduce daily calorie intake.

FUTURE STEPS LEADING TO THE GOAL:

1.   Join an athletic facility.

2.   Reward myself with an evening out for every 10 pounds lost.

3.   Share my progress with others.

In an effort to insure that he carefully thought the goal through, he listed at least two positive and two negative aspects involved in undertaking the goal. For example, under the goal listed above, the positive aspects included:

1.   Improve self-image

2.   Development of self-discipline

The negative side included:

1.   Will take self-discipline

2.   Diet behavior must be modified

For some goals, he experienced ease in listing the positive and negative sides. For others, the process was very difficult. In either case he found the exercise insightful. It helped him to understand better the challenges which lay ahead.

Understanding human nature, he recognized that his intentions, regardless of how well he had thought them out, might not become a reality in their intended form. If exceptionally favorable circumstances presented themselves and he easily reached his goals, he would need further challenges toward which to work. If everything seemed to go wrong even though he had given proper time and effort to reaching the goal, he needed to be able to at least reach the minimum level. In an effort to make these allowances, he established levels of Minimum Acceptable Accomplishment and Maximum Expected Accomplishment. To support his weight loss goal he stated the maximum and minimum goal levels as follows:

MAXIMUM EXPECTED ACCOMPLISHMENT:

Establish and maintain a weight of 150 pounds.

MINIMUM ACCEPTABLE ACCOMPLISHMENT:

Establish and maintain a weight of 165 pounds.

Because he had a specific written goal and steps to steer him toward that goal, he exceeded the stated minimum goal and came close to reaching the maximum expected accomplishment.

The year was a time of tremendous growth. Comparing this period with the past, the young man was amazed at the increased productivity and personal development which transpired. He contributed the effectiveness of the approach to 'harnessed energies' which now had an 'orderly' direction (I Corinthians 14:40).

When first embarking on a major project such as this, there are often frustrations which emerge. For this person, discipline and consistency ranked high. Some of the superficial goals went by the wayside. Unless he believed in the goals and felt that they were realistic and worthwhile, he found them very difficult to attain.

After discussing his project with others who had also written goals, he discovered that it was best to have one major goal or theme for the year and several minor ones. He found that when he tried to place the same emphasis in each area of his life, his thoughts and priorities were divided. When other goals were structured to complement the main theme and goal, they worked together rather than against one another. For example, during the first year of his experience, he emphasized weight loss. He developed friendships at the athletic club and became active on a church athletic team. In this way, goals in the social, mental, spiritual and ministry areas supported his major goal. In subsequent years, he ranked goals in other areas as high, placing them as his priority. Supporting goals then complemented this major thrust.

A yearly theme was ultimately integrated into the process, keying in on a major theme for the year. Yearly themes eventually included: 'How close I can get to God?', 'I can do all things through Christ my strength', 'Recognition through innovation', 'In the process of becoming', and 'A year for change'. He also added verses to support his yearly themes.

This exercise of establishing themes, goals and steps for carrying out the goals to completion is essential. Unless action is taken to 'bridge the gap' between where a person is today and where he believes God would have him in the future, the preceding chapters are of little value.

Establishing personal goals should entail a great deal of contemplation and introspection. It should not be attempted in one sitting. Then, a basic statement describing purpose for being (Life Theme) should be written.

In establishing themes and goals, people should take both a *micro* and a *macro* view of their lives. The *micro* view is one which allows a person the freedom to let their minds explore the many possibilities which exist for their lives. This exploration is confined or narrow in that it concentrates on the individual and negates the restraints of existing responsibilities to others as well as personal skills and abilities. For example, the person who gives his total energies to the needs of his job may find that he is neglecting to have any leisure time. An evening with the family, several days fishing or even physical exercise may seem like a luxury. The micro disregards his current situation and lets his imagination run free. He may envision a week-long fishing expedition with the family, an ocean cruise, or his own 20-foot fishing vessel.

Included in such dreaming should be the most outlandish wishes and fantasies. Listed should be whatever comes to mind. While this could seem embarrassing or silly, these dreams are a part of your inner thoughts and they should be written down so you can see what they are. After all, God already knows about them so it is not up to you anyway. Bob Pierce, the founder and former president of World Vision International used to caution his staff to 'Leave God room' in their planning. As children of God, we should have confidence that God can do great things through our lives.

People should consider each area of their lives. They will be most creative if they allow themselves not to be bound by their current responsibilities. They should allow their minds to run free and consider the many options available to them. Just like the young executive, they should keep notes concerning their thoughts and dream goals. These will help them in the next stage of the goal-making process. This step is called the *macro* view.

The macro view entails a vision of personal goals in light of the personal abilities and effect of goals upon others. For example, the mother who wishes to begin a career outside the home will need to consider the impact of such a move upon her children. Additional finances and professional growth may be advantageous, but the need for day care and quality time with her husband may be overriding. By weighing the different factors involved, the mother will be better able to make a responsible decision. She may decide that, due to the nature of her work and/or family situation, career involvement is right for her. Conversely, she may feel that it is more important for her to stay at home with her children. A compromise consisting of either part-time work or career postponement for several years might also be considered.

The process of narrowing down the options to those choices which are most responsible and God-honoring is called suboptiminization. Suboptiminization is the process of selecting what may not be ideal or 'optimum' for the individual, but the wisest and most responsible choice when considering the influence of the decision upon others. The parent, for example, who spends the child's school clothes money at the bowling alley has only taken a micro view and determined to do that which will bring him optimum pleasure. Conversely, the parent who sacrifices his enjoyment of bowling so that his children can have shoes for school has taken a macro view of the situation and selected the option which is suboptimum for him, but is best for everyone involved.

Once responsible objectives and goals have been established, realistic steps can be written which will lead to their completion. This process of establishing life priorities and setting realistic procedures for reaching them will only be effective when accompanied with fervent prayer. A person must truly believe that these goals reflect God's will for him. Half-hearted goals will seldom be achieved. Seeing goals through to reality requires tenacity, hard work and discipline.

The Apostle Paul is a fine example of someone who established God-centered goals. First he set a general *aim* for his life. This aim was to 'press on toward the goal to win the prize for which God has called me heavenward in Christ

Jesus' (Philippians 3:14 - NIV). He then set specific *goals* leading to that aim: '... after I have completed this task ... I will go to Spain and visit you on the way' (Romans 15:28 - NIV). Even after he prayerfully set his goals, he remained attune to the leading of the Holy Spirit (Acts 16:7) in order that the Lord would be glorified in all that he said or did (I Corinthians 10:31). Paul was a man who accomplished much. Had he not dedicated himself to a general aim, to specific goals which supported that aim, and to the leading of the Holy Spirit, he might not have made the tremendous impact upon Christianity which he did.

Paul knew who he was and what he wanted to do with his life. As children in the royal family of God, today's Christians should also feel a responsibility to learn the abilities which God has given to them. They can then select a direction in which to develop these qualities so that they can be used for the honor and glory of the King.

CONCLUSION

CONCLUSION

Personal development is not easy. It requires a systematic process including balanced and healthful introspection, the creation of both long and short term goals, and the tenacity to carry out the tasks needed to reach each objective. The ultimate aim of all that we do should be to glorify God through personal depth and lives that are properly balanced.

Character development is not achieved overnight. It is a long-term process which has been likened to a marathon runner. This athlete is not like the sprinter who quickly dashes toward his goal and is finished in a few moments. The marathon runner starts the race at a balanced pace. His stride is swift enough to insure competition and tempered so that he will not tire and be unable to finish. Mile after mile he travels, maintaining his even pace.

Character development is a process which should encompass a Christian's entire life. As he progresses through life, difficult times emerge. The person who learns to work through each situation in a well-paced and natural process will, like the marathon runner, be able to hold his pace until the end of the race. The person who tries to sprint the marathon will quickly burn out and never reach his goal. This type of systematic, long-term development is the intent of this study.

Of necessity, personal growth requires discipline and direction. Discipline provides the endurance needed to continue through the many difficulties which are inherent to growth. Direction puts the energies in a productive channel.

Challenges and difficulties are an intrinsic part of personal growth. Because of the character development which results from such circumstances, Paul encourages believers to have a good attitude about them. He writes, '... we also rejoice in our sufferings, because we know that suffering produces perseverance; perseverance, character; and character hope' (Romans 5:3-4 - NIV).

In the book of James we find:

> *'Consider it pure joy, by brothers, whenever you face trials of many kinds, because you know that the testing of your faith develops perseverance. Perseverance must finish its work so that you may be mature and complete, not lacking anything' (James 1:2-4 - NIV).*

Personal growth and development are epitomized in these two verses. It only occurs as the result of hard work guided in a healthful direction. The end result of such an emphasis should be the enhancement of the fruits of the Spirit (love, joy, peace, patience, kindness, goodness, faithfulness, gentleness and self-control - Galatians 5:22-23 - NIV), and ultimately the glorification of God.

This book has been developed with this intent. The ultimate responsibility, however, lies with each individual who participates in the program. Merely reading the material is insufficient. Contemplation and application to a person's life maximizes its effectiveness in their personal lives, the lives of their families, and their ministry areas.

APPENDIX:

EXERCISES FOR FURTHER
DEVELOPMENT:

BIBLICAL OVERVIEW

1. What is your purpose for reading through this material on personal growth and development?

2. Using Biblical principles, support the hypothesis that Christian men and women should develop the talents and abilities given to them by God.

3. Do you believe that personal development is a continual responsibility for every Christian? Explain.

    A.   Summarize what you would like to gain through reading this book.

    B.   How would you like it to affect your family life?

    C.   How would you like it to affect your ministry?

4. Make a list of five talents or characteristics which God has given to you. Explain how you have used these to glorify Him in the past.

5. Do you agree or disagree with the statement, 'There ain't no free lunch' as it is presented in the context of this material? Give evidence to support your answer.

6. Review Matthew 25:14-30. If the Lord were to return today, which of the three servants would most accurately reflect you? Explain, providing illustrations to support your answer.

7. How might pride interfere with the fruitfulness of your Christian life?

8. In what way might excessive humility impair the effectiveness of your Christian life?

9. What implications does I Corinthians 10:31 have for personal growth and development?

10. In light of Proverbs 16:9, I Corinthians 14:40 and Philippians 3:13-14 respond to the statement, 'God made me the way that I am. If He wants me to develop or change, He will have to do it.'

11. Review the lives of Joseph, Job, Daniel and David.

   A.   For each man cite at least three ways in which they developed their character.

   B.   How would Jewish history have been altered if they had not developed their character?

12. Read Romans 8:16-21; Galatians 3:26-29; Ephesians 1:11-12; I Peter 1:3-5; and I John 3:1-3.

   A.   Who are the children of God?

   B.   Describe their rights and responsibilities.

   C.   How does a royal position in the household of God relate to the Christian's responsibility for personal growth?

RECOGNIZING OUR PERSONAL RESPONSIBILITY

1. Humanists say that man is in control of his destiny. Other people say that all of life is controlled by fate. Read carefully Ephesians 5:15,16. What responsibility does the scriptures say you have over your future?

2. Who was Pyrrhus? What can we learn from him about our ability to control our future?

3. The Apostle Paul is described as a man who had a 'yes' face. What does this mean?

   A.   List some of the limitations that he had in his life.

   B.   Indicate some of the ways God used him to help establish the early church.

4. Consider the statement, 'Dreaming and doing must go hand in hand.' Give the rational for why both are important.

5. Peter Tchaikovsky is described as someone who stayed the course in spite of difficult circumstances. Recount the example given in the text. What are some of the challenges you face in your life? What steps can you take to overcome them?

6. Read carefully Ephesians 5:15,16. What does it mean to make the best of every opportunity? How should this be seen in your life?

7. It has been said that it is not past successes or failures but today's performance that counts. What is meant by this? How should this influence the way in which you approach your daily activities?

8. As a Christian you have one central responsibility to maintain throughout your life (Matthew 22:36-38). What is this responsibility? How should it influence your priorities, decisions and actions?

9. A close friendship with God that is continually nurtured is essential to maintain a Christian focus. Describe the steps you can take daily to build your relationships with the Lord.

10. What is excellence?

   A.   Do you believe that every believer should be the best that he can be in every aspect of his life? Explain your rational.

   B.   What role should the concept of balanced priorities play in a person's life? Consider the importance of the proper balance between spiritual, social, physical, occupational, intellectual and family priorities.

RECOGNIZING THE NEED/
REALIZING THE CHALLENGE

1. How can an honest self-awareness help you become a more effective servant of God? Provide at least one illustration to support your answer.

2. Peer back through the pages of your life history. Describe three ways in which you have changed during the past five years. Are these changes healthy or unhealthy? Explain.

3. At the top of a sheet of paper write 'Who am I?' Below, number from 1 to 50. Finish the sentence 'I am...' with fifty different responses. Quickly jot down whatever comes to mind. Be very honest with yourself. You are the only one who will see your list. Now answer each of the following questions.

    A.   What did this indicate about the types of roles you play in life?

    B.   What was revealed about your inner character?

    C.   Did you find that completing this list was easy or difficult? Explain.

    D.   Did some of your responses seem to contradict others? What explanation do you have for this?

    E.   Were more of your responses positive or negative? What conclusion can you draw from this?

F. List three observations which you have made about yourself which resulted from this exercise.

4. Divide a sheet of paper into two columns. On the left, write a 'Victory List' describing at least 50 of your qualities or accomplishments. On the right hand column, list 25 characteristics which you believe to be limiting or negative factors.

A. Which list was easiest for you to write? Why do you believe it was easiest to write?

B. Did these lists help you to understand yourself better? Why or why not?

C. Review carefully the content of your lists, giving special attention to qualities and accomplishments which are germane to both columns. Then answer each of the following questions:

1. What does this tell you about your natural abilities and your basic interests?

2. What does this say about your liabilities or areas in which you may want to limit your involvement?

3. On what areas might you want to concentrate your future development?

5. Can a person ever gain a complete understanding of himself? Why or why not?

6. In what ways can self-awareness help a Christian to better understand and to minister to the needs of *others*?

7. What are two basic ways a person can respond to change? Which do you believe is the most healthful? Explain.

8. List at least five things which influence your total make-up as a person. Write a short paragraph for each one, sharing how they influence the development of your character.

9. Write a brief (10 pages or less) diary of your entire life. This should be an informal essay of where you have been, what you have done, where you were working, how you have felt. It should include each aspect of your life from the time you were a small infant until now.

  A. Are there special people, places or things which have influenced you to become what or who you are today? Explain.

  B. What did you learn about the talents, abilities and skills which you possess?

  C. What talents, abilities or skills could you develop to an even greater extent? Is this practical? In what way would this enhance your life?

RUNNING THE RISK

1. In what way is trying to gain a truthful understanding of one's self a 'risk'?

2. In what ways are inhibitions a healthy part of a person's make-up?

3. How can inhibitions be harmful to a person's life?

4. Do you believe that the person you portray to others *always* reflects the real you? Explain, citing examples to illustrate your points.

5. Review questions numbered three and four in the chapter 'Recognizing the Need/ Realizing the Challenge'.

    A.   What are your feelings about sharing these lists with others?

    B.   Do you feel threatened or enlightened by the thought of others reading them? Explain.

    C.   If you are able, show your responses to a trusted friend.

        1.   Did they agree with your list or do they feel that the list should be altered? Explain their response.

        2.   Do you agree with their analysis? Why or why not?

3.   If you did not share your response
     with someone else, write 250 words
     explaining why.

6. Define the words 'individuality' and 'conformity'.

   A.   What are the major distinctions between the
        meanings of these two words?

   B.   How can an excessive amount of either of
        these qualities be harmful?

   C.   How can a lack of either one be harmful?

   D.   Describe how each of these words should
        ideally fit into your life.

7. Describe some of the masks you have hidden behind.
   Were some healthy? Explain. Were some harmful?
   Why?

8. Do you think you could handle the trauma of finding
   out that your past view of yourself is inaccurate?
   Explain.

9. Define the word 'entrepreneur'. How could this
   concept prove helpful to the Christian life?

10. Define the word 'failure'. How does it affect a
    person differently than success?

11. Respond in writing to the statement, 'Conformers
    are people who do not want to think for themselves.'

REMAINING REALISTIC

1. Relate the words 'sober judgment' to the intent of Romans 12:3.

2. Why is it important to have a realistic view of oneself? How could an elevated or depressed understanding create problems with a person's relationships with others? Use true-to-life illustrations to support your answer.

3. In what ways are rationalizations temporarily helpful?

4. How can rationalizations be harmful? Illustrate your response.

5. Write a description for three of the major roles you play in life (i.e. father/mother, teacher, spouse, camp director, pastor, counselor, hostess/host, etc.). Include each of the following in your description.

   A.   Name of the role.

   B.   Indicate your qualifications. Include natural abilities, interests, skills, experience and training.

   C.   Carefully examine the scope and thrust of what you do. In a sentence or two indicate what you do and an overview of your basic areas of responsibility.

   D.   Are you satisfied with your performance in each of these roles? Explain.

6. Describe several areas of your life in which you think you might be rationalizing today.

   A.   In general terms, why do you think you have rationalized in these areas?

   B.   Is your rationalization healthy or harmful? In what ways?

7. If you do not believe that you rationalize any of your actions or thoughts, share this conviction with your spouse or a close friend. Did they agree? What did they indicate was the reasoning for their response? Do you agree with them? Has this encounter influenced your relationship with them in any way? Explain.

8. Do you believe that you currently have a realistic understanding of who you are as a person? Give evidence to support your answer.

REFLECTION, RE-EVALUATION, AND RE-INTERPRETATION

1. What role do you believe a personal quiet time should play in your life? Is this true for you today?

2. Describe your plan of action for insuring that you have adequate time for reflection, re-evaluation and re-interpretation. If you have not developed one, do so.

3. Describe the structure of a quiet time. What changes would you need to make if you were to alter your current time of meditation to fit the structure you described?

4. Why do you think Nehemiah spent four months in thought and meditation before rebuilding the walls of Jerusalem?

5. Of what significance is the quality of advice to proper decision making?

6. What is 'stimulus flooding'? Has this been evidenced in your life? Explain.

7. Why is it sometimes important to 'let things set' before taking action?

RELATIONSHIPS WITH OTHERS

1. Do you have someone who is close to you and with whom you can 'talk things through'?

   A.   Is this healthy or unhealthy? Why?

   B.   How can this relationship influence your life and ministry?

2. What characteristics should a person possess before you consider placing your confidence in him?

3. What advice would you give to someone who was trying to find someone with whom to talk through things?

4. How does the concept of 'clearing the fog' by talking with others correlate with reflection, re-evaluation and re-interpretation?

5. Have you ever experienced a time when you needed someone with whom to talk through things, but there was no one around to fill the need? If so, explain your feelings. If not, talk with several others until you find someone else who has. Explain the feelings they expressed.

6. In light of this subject describe the relationship between David and Jonathan. Do you believe their opportunity to 'talk through things' enhanced their character growth? Explain.

RESISTING EXCESSIVE INTROSPECTION

1. Review the words 'morbid' and 'introspection' as they appear in the dictionary. Based upon these definitions and your understanding of the term 'morbid introspection' as it is used in this chapter, write your own definition for it.

2. What dangers exist in excessive introspection?

3. Why is a balanced amount of personal introspection important?

4. What would your advice be to someone who was depressed because of morbid introspection in their life?

5. Christ demonstrated a balance between time spent alone in thought and prayer and time helping others. List several scriptures which support these actions, explaining each situation in your own words.

6. Reread the poem about the centipede. What application can this poem have to your life?

7. As a result of your own experience, exposure to others, reading and research, write a 'true to life' illustration of morbid introspection. Was this situation ever alleviated? If so, how? If not, why not?

8. What personal or ministry-related application can you make from the experience described in question seven?

REFUSING COMPARISON

1. Why do you believe that the Lord made each person uniquely different from anyone else? Give evidence to support your response.

2. Why do you believe Christian men and women compare themselves with others?

3. Examine Ephesians 4:1-13. What basic principle is conveyed which can be applied to the concept of comparison?

4. Comparison can be used to make a person feel proud. Explain the influence of this action upon the person's relationship with the one to whom he has compared himself.

5. Is it possible for comparison to ever be healthy? Explain your answer.

6. List four heroes or people you could or do admire.

   A.   List three outstanding qualities for each one.

   B.   What similar characteristics prevail between them?

   C.   Write a paragraph describing the importance that these people have been to your life.

   D.   Do you believe that you compare yourself to these people in an unhealthy way? Explain.

   E.   Do you believe that heroes are important for people to have? Why or why not?

7. Team up with someone and spend a day or an evening in the skid row or ghetto part of a city. Sincerely ask questions of some of the people you meet about life and their lifestyle. Some will give you an honest response, others will not.

   A.   What feelings do you have about their lifestyles in general?

B. Do you feel that you are better off as far as a total lifestyle is concerned? Explain.

C. In what way was this exercise helpful to your understanding of yourself or appreciation of your life?

D. In what way could this exercise be harmful to you or to others?

E. Equate what you did in this exercise with II Corinthians 10:12. What conclusions can you draw?

REWARDS OF PERSONAL HANDICAPS

1. Make a list of at least five things which you consider to be weaknesses in your life.

A. In what ways do these limit you?

B. How have you compensated for them in the past?

C. Each one can result in bringing you strength either in character, spirituality, skills, or physically. Explain how this is true for each of the weaknesses you listed.

2. Make a list of at least five things which you consider to be strengths in your life.

A.   In what ways do these provide expanded
      opportunities for you?

B.   How have you developed them in the past?

C.   What strengths of character, skills or physical
      assets have emerged from each of these
      qualities?

3. In II Corinthians 12:10, what does Paul mean when
   he states, 'I am content with my weaknesses'?

4. In what ways can handicaps or weaknesses help to
   make a person stronger?

5. Reflect upon the quotation from Helen Keller. In
   what way can this statement apply to your life?

6. Review the life of the Apostle Paul. Show at least
   two situations where he was able to use physical or
   situational limitations to his advantage.

7. Moses was 'slow in speech'. What was the Lord's
   response to Moses when Moses mentioned this to
   God? What was its ultimate impact upon the
   effectiveness of Moses' mission and ministry?

PERSONAL ESTEEM FROM A BIBLICAL PERSPECTIVE

1. Define the term 'personal esteem'. Use Romans 12:3 as the basis of your definition.

2. In I Corinthians 15:9-10, Paul states, 'But by the grace of God I am what I am.' (NIV)

   A. Explain the substance of this statement.

   B. From what source does a child of God receive his value? Explain.

   C. Do you believe Paul had a 'realistic understanding' of who he was? Give scripture to support your answer.

3. What role does humility play in healthy personal esteem?

4. How does God show his personal interest in the unbeliever even before his birth? (Psalm 139:13-16).

5. In what ways has God demonstrated your value to Him? Use scripture to support your answer.

6. In Matthew 6:26 we encounter Jesus' insights: 'Look at the birds of the air; they do not sow or reap or store away in barns, and yet your heavenly Father feeds them. Are you not much more valuable than they?' (NIV) Interpret Christ's question, 'Are you not much more valuable than they?'

PERSONAL LOVE FOR OTHERS

1. Write your own definition for love.

2. Based upon your own definition, are you a loving person?

3. Is it important for a person to feel loved by everyone? Explain.

4. Who are the 'significant others' in your life? Give evidence to support your conclusion.

5. Compare two persons with whom you are acquainted who are different in their ability to love or to show love to others. One of these people may be yourself. What do you think accounts for this difference?

6 Jesus said to 'love thy neighbor *as thyself*.' What influence should this place upon a Christian's feelings about himself?

7. What is meant by a 'shortage of love'? Provide true life examples to support your response.

8. Why is it important for people to fill any shortage of love in their lives?

9. Some people demonstrate a *need* to be at the center of attention.

   A. How does this differ from people who *appreciate* or *enjoy* attention?

B.   What relation do you see between people who *need* attention and people who *fear* it?

10. What steps can you take to help other people who might feel a shortage of love in their lives?

11. What steps could you take to help members of your *own* family who feel a shortage of love in their lives?

12. Is it possible to give a child too much love? Explain.

13. Imagine you are at a picnic. People are gathered in groups based upon their interests.

A.   Write a paragraph which describes the characteristics of the people in the group that you would be most likely to join.

B.   Describe the people in the group from which you would be most repelled.

C.   Define the word 'homogeneous'. How does it relate to any conclusions you might draw about your relationships with the groups described in A and B?

14. Not every Christian is able to get along well with others.

A.   Explain the ramifications this can have upon your ministry to others.

B.   In what ways can this influence your family?

PERSONAL IMAGE

1. Review your responses to the exercises in the chapters 'Realizing the Challenge' and 'Remaining Realistic'. Write a description of who you are. Include a paragraph on each aspect of your life (spiritual, mental, social, physical, family, ministry). Be truthful, listing both the good with the not so good.

    A.   Did you like everything that you found? Explain.

    B.   Do you believe that you were totally honest with yourself? How is this evidenced?

    C.   What did you learn about yourself as a result of this exercise?

2. Each person plays different roles in life. The same man may be a pastor, counselor, client, disciplinarian, and husband all in the same day.

    A.   How do you think these different roles influence the image you have of yourself?

    B.   Do you believe these roles influence the image you have of yourself? Why or why not?

3. Do you think that others see you differently than you really are? Explain. What influence could this have upon your relationship with them?

4. Indicate the influences your self-image will have upon your effectiveness in each of the following (respond only to those which apply to you):

   A.   Your ministry to others.

   B.   As a parent.

   C.   As a spouse.

   D.   Socially.

5. For most people, the image that they have of themselves changes over the years. In what ways do you see yourself differently today than you did ten years ago?

6. Is your current image of yourself consistent with what you would like it to be? Explain. If not, write a descriptive paragraph of the self-image you would like to have.

7. What influences can your self-image have upon your reaction to others and the effectiveness of your ministry?

8. If married, write a job description for your role as a father/mother and then one as a husband/wife. Determine the correct amount of time which should be spent in each area.

   A.   What criteria did you use to determine this time? Why?

B.   What elements will influence changes in this amount of time over the next few years?

9. What is the relationship between the way you believe you look physically (body image) and your self-image or self-esteem?

10. What effect does *your* 'body image' have upon your personality and behavior?

11. Compare your 'body image' and your 'body ideal'. What effect does the discrepancy between these two have on you?

12. Describe your efforts at dress, exercise, diet, etc. which are aimed at enhancing your appearance. Do you think that this is important? Why or why not?

13. Do other people's body appearance or body build influence your response to them? Explain.

PERSONAL ACCEPTANCE

1. In what ways should the approval of others be important to you?

2. In what sense should the approbation of others be of little value to you?

3. Define the term 'other-worth'. Write a series of paragraphs indicating the significance it has played in your life in the following areas:

A. Your home church.

B. The car you drive.

C. The way you discipline your children.

D. What you order when you dine out.

E. The clothes you wear.

F. The way you handle yourself when preaching or teaching.

G. The way you pray publicly.

H. The way you respond toward people you find it difficult to like.

I. Your personal conversations with others.

4. While attending high school, some of the students in your class were more popular than others.

A. What influence do you think the actions of the more popular students might have had upon the feelings of inferiority of the less popular students?

B. What personal application can you draw from your conclusion in 'A'? Include both your actions toward others, the actions of others toward you, and the resulting feelings of both.

5. Almost everyone is sensitive to the approval and disapproval of the people who play 'important' roles in their life. Who are these 'important' people in your life?

6. What importance does the approbation by a 'significant other' have in a person's acceptance of himself?

   A.   How can this be related to child-rearing?

   B.   What significance can this have in the husband-wife relationships?

7. Review the varied roles you have played (i.e. student, teacher, parent, child). What influence did the expectations of others have upon the way you felt about yourself?

8. How do you feel around people whom you regard as superior? Do you feel less than adequate around them? How does this affect your actions?

9. It was once stated, 'I am often influenced by what others think of me. When the opinions of others contradicts who I think I am, this causes frustration and internal conflict.' What can the Christian do to relieve this situation?

10. Contemplate the saying, 'nothing to prove, nothing to lose'. In some ways this statement is healthy and in some ways it is not. Discuss your opinion.

11. Do you agree with the statement, 'I'm me, and I'm good, 'cause God don't make junk?' Explain, using scripture to support your answer.

PERSONAL POTENTIAL

1. 'People need to be moving ahead in life, or they will become stagnant.' Comment on this statement. How does it relate to your philosophy of life?

2. Do you believe that you are living up to your personal potential? Explain.

3. List the spiritual gifts that God has entrusted to you. For each one indicate:

   A.   If you are satisfied with the way they are being used. Explain your reasoning.

   B.   How you are developing and refining them so that you can be an even more effective servant of God.

4. Do you think you have acquired a full appreciation of the abilities and opportunities which have been entrusted to you? Explain, giving illustrations to support your answer.

5. How have you changed in the past few years? Do you believe this change is 'growth'? Explain your answer.

6. Do you feel that your concept of yourself is 'frozen' or in some way prevents you from growing? Explain.

7. In the eyes of God, are the gifts and talents you possess more important than those He has given to others? Explain, using scriptures to support your response.

8. To what extent have you realized your potential?

9. Write a minimum of two pages explaining your convictions about the value and potential of the gifts which Christ has given to you.

10. What is your assessment of the statements, 'Middle age is the prime of life,' and 'Life begins at forty?' In what way do they support the concept that a person should always be growing?

PERSONAL PROBLEMS

1. List the steps which contributed to Elijah's recovery from depression.

2. As stated in the text, it has been estimated that 90% of the things which people worry about never actually transpire. Do you believe this to be true in your own life? Explain.

3. Is there a difference between sincere concern and anxiety? Explain, providing examples to support your answer.

4. Using the format below, make a list of at least five things you could or do worry about. Cite the worst possible thing which could happen in each situation and then note the best possible outcome. Finally indicate what you think is the most probable outcome.

Problem_____

_____

_____

Worst outcome ____ ____ ____ ____ ____ ____ ____

Best outcome ____ ____ ____ ____ ____ ____ ___

Probable outcome ____ ____ ____ ____ ____ ___

What did you learn from this exercise which might be helpful to you in the future?

5. Explain the concept of 'day tight compartments'. Can they be helpful in dealing with anxiety? Explain.

6. Why is it important for people to have inner peace if they wish to help others?

7. What aspects of your life could lead to stress overload? What steps can you take to help relieve this?

8. Do you believe that Christians who are in fellowship with God are exempt from mental distress? Explain.

9. Is depression always the result of sin? Explain.

10. Respond to the statement, 'Sometimes depression can be the most healthy response to a situation.' Do you agree with this statement? Explain.

11. What should the attitude of the church be toward people who experience problems related to mental stress?

12. What are some of the physical imbalances which can lead to mental stress? What can be done to help alleviate this?

13. List the guidelines in Philippians 4:6-9 which deal with overcoming anxiety. How do they relate to the actions taken by Jehosophat in II Chronicles 20:1-30?

14. Read the following scriptures. Of what value can each verse be in times of trouble?

Exodus 33:19   Psalm 31:9   Psalm 86:5
Exodus 34:6   Psalm 34:8   Psalm 106:1
Psalm 145:7   Psalm 27:13   Psalm 107:8-9
Psalm 65:4   James 1:17

15. What is your most persistent temptation? Why is it so difficult to say no to this temptation?

16. After careful contemplation, answer the following question: Do you have an accurate and practical view of God's loving concern for you and His desire to meet your needs?

PERSONAL HAPPINESS

1. Write your own definition for happiness.

2. Is happiness something a healthy Christian should experience at all times? Explain your reasoning.

3. Epictetus wrote, 'If a man is unhappy, his unhappiness is his own fault.' Defend or refute this statement, providing evidence to support your answer.

4. Are you generally a happy person? Give personal illustrations to support your response.

5. What general advice would you give to a fellow Christian who indicated to you that he was not a happy person?

6. To you, what are the basic differences between work and play? How do these qualities relate to your ministry involvement?

7. Do you agree or disagree with the saying, 'Happiness is a perfume you cannot pour on others without getting a few drops on yourself?' Explain using illustrations to support your answer.

8. What activities are or could prove to be recreative for you? Do you regularly participate in such? Why or why not?

9. Do you consider happiness to be an important,

possible, or worthy goal? Explain your response.

10. Can you be happy in some things and, at the same time, not be happy in others? Explain.

11. Describe the difference between joy and contentment. How do these two words relate to the term happiness?

12. Describe a recent 'peak experience' you had. Did you have control over either the situation or your reaction to it? Explain.

13. Describe a recent 'low experience' you had. Did you have control over either the situation or your reaction to it? Explain.

14. What general conclusions can you make about happiness as a result of reading the following scriptures:

> Psalm 118:24   Galatians 5:22,23
> Ecclesiastes 3:1-8   Ephesians 4:23
> Mark 8:34,36   Philippians 4:4
> John 10:10   Philippians 4:8
> Romans 15:2

15. Compare your present general level of happiness with the levels that were characteristic of your earlier stages of life.

   A.   Are you happier now than you were before? Explain.

B.   Do you expect to be happier in the later stages of your life? Why or why not?

16. Make a lengthy and detailed list of the things which make you happy. Include at least 50 items. Divide your list into two columns.

1.   In the first column, list the things which are under your control.

2.   In the second, place the things which lie under the control of others, fate, or circumstance.

3.   Review your lists for accuracy. Then decide whether you should place your priorities upon altering your external environment (work, home, and/or friends) or your internal self (attitude, personal growth, spiritual life, skills in interpersonal relationships).

4.   List specific goals for making necessary alterations. Be sure to include a time frame for both beginning and completing work on these goals.

17. In a hundred words or more, describe your personal satisfaction as it pertains to each of the following:

Home Life   Material Goods
Personal Growth   Spiritual Growth
Ministry Effectiveness   Physical Characteristics
Relationships with Others

PERSONAL VALUES

1. Define the word 'value' in your own words.

2. In what sense should each Christian have values which are the same as all other believers? In what sense should each Christian have values which are unique to him or her?

   A.   List some of the values which should remain uniform.

   B.   Write several values which are distinctly yours.

3. Will a person's actions reflect his true values? Explain.

4. Take a close look at your job, family, friendships, health, and possessions. List the ten actions and/or possessions which you value most. Do you believe that the amount of time you spend on each item reflects the value you place upon it? Explain your reasoning. If not, should the emphasis of your time be altered? Explain.

5. In what sense does the word 'holistic' fit into the theme of the chapter?

6. Describe the family you were reared in and your perception of its effect upon your values.

7. Compare your values with those of your parents or

guardian as a child. How are they different? How are they the same?

8. What rights or freedoms were you denied as a child which might have proven desirable or beneficial? Justify your response.

9. What rights or freedoms which were denied you as a child are you now extending or planning to extend to your own children? Explain.

10. Which five of the following values *actually* hold the most attraction for you? Indicate why.

Achievement	Belongingness
Security	Affection
Glamor	Service
Approval	Power
Status	Authority
Wealth	

11. Describe the thing which you feel is most sacred to your life. This may be your family, spouse, feelings of being truthful, love of the arts, or anything that you truly hold to be sacred. Have you ever tended to take it for granted? If not, why not? If so, how could this be avoided in the future?

12. What is it that, if you lost it, life would have no meaning? Why do you think this is so?

RESPONSIBILITY FOR GROWTH

1. In what sense do you believe that Christians are responsible for their own actions? How does this relate to their personal growth and development?

2. What roles do tenacity, hard work and discipline play in personal growth? Provide a true-life illustration to support your answer.

3. Explain the concept of the 'ifs' of life as it appears in this study. List some of the 'ifs' you have used in the past. Were they valid? Why or why not?

4. Are your mate, family or friends in any way responsible for the direction, intensity and speed of your personal growth? Explain, using the life of Joseph as found in Genesis 39:21-23 to support your answer.

5. Share in detail both your feelings and the events which surrounded a personal growth spurt.

   A.   In what sense were you responsible for this growth?

   B.   What are the chances that you will experience a similar growth spurt again in the future?

6. If you continue developing as you have, who do you expect to be ten years from now? Twenty years from now? Are you satisfied with this prospect? Why or why not?

7. Who would you be ten years from now if you quite fully realized your potential? Twenty years from now? What might keep you from becoming this person?

8. Read David's prayer of repentance for his sin with Bathsheba (Psalm 51).

   A.   What evidence is there that David took full responsibility for his actions?

   B.   Read Romans 1:18-32. Trace the spiral of sin by asking, 'Why is man responsible for his behavior?'

9. Examine the excuses of Moses:

Excuse of Insignificance	Exodus 3:11
Excuse of Ignorance	Exodus 3:13
Excuse of Inadequacy	Exodus 4:1
Excuse of Inability	Exodus 4:10
Excuse of Indifference	Exodus 4:13

   A.   In what sense was each excuse valid?

   B.   In what sense was each one not valid?

   C.   What practical application can you draw from the example of Moses?

FOUNDATION FOR GROWTH

1. Write your reaction to I Timothy 4:14a ('Neglect not the gift that is in thee...' - KJV) as it pertains to your personal development.

2. How does the old saying 'You can't teach an old dog new tricks' relate to your personal development?

3. What is a Comfort Zone? Does everyone have one?

4. Describe the perimeters of your Comfort Zone.

5. What are some specific things you can do to foster growth and avoid stagnation in your own life?

6. Read I Corinthians 14:40. How does this verse apply to the process of expanding a Comfort Zone?

7. Define the terms *Growth Motivation* and *Deficiency Motivation*.

   A.   What are the distinguishing principles which separate these two?

   B.   Which of these two types of motivation generally provide the stimuli for you to grow or change?

8. What role does a person's attitude play in the effectiveness of his or her personal development?

9. Why is it unlikely that a person will experience a

perfect balance between attitude, knowledge and skill? Give an example to substantiate your response.

10. Make a list of ten strengths or talents which you possess.

    A.   Write five possible ways you can develop each one.

    B.   Are you going to develop any of these talents with the suggestions listed? Why or why not?

11. Which of the following reflects your belief about the learning abilities of 'middle-agers'?

    A.   Not as able as before.

    B.   More knowledge to which to tie new ideas.

    C.   Other.

Write fifty words or more to substantiate your response.

BLUEPRINT FOR GROWTH

1. What is a 'blueprint for life'?

2. Are there some aspects of a 'blueprint for life' which are unalterable? Explain.

3. What influence does a person's self-image have upon his life map?

4. In a paragraph or more, discuss at least three of the people who have most influenced your maturation. Explain the ways in which this growth occurred.

5. Do you believe that your personality is inherited, an effect of your planning, learned from your parents, the result of your experiences or a combination of these? Explain your reasoning.

6. Describe the significance of early life influences on the total blueprint for life.

7. How did your immediate family influence your blueprint for growth?

8. Can society in general affect a blueprint for life? Explain.

9. What are some of the ways the Lord influences a person's life map?

10. Was the college freshman described by Coach Mudra *responsible* for his early scholastic failure or a *victim* of an ill-designed blueprint? Provide a thorough explanation of your reasoning.

11. Write a drama of your own blueprint for life. Include in each act significant events which helped to shape your attitudes, growth and major choices.

Act I	Early Childhood
Act II	Adolescence
Act III	18-30
Act IV	31-50
Act V	50-70
Act VI	70-Final Curtain

A.   Cite at least ten insights which you gained about the events and people who helped to shape you as a person.

B.   Of what value can these insights be as you make plans to shape your future?

12. Do you have an internal voice that drives you to produce? Is this healthy or not? Explain your reasoning.

ENVIRONMENT FOR GROWTH

1. Describe the home environment in which you were brought up. Tell about the house or homes, relationships with your brothers and/or sisters, neighbors, parents, teachers, etc.

A.   What aspects of this environment do you reject in your own life today?

B.   Which aspects do you cherish? Why?

2. Of what significance do you believe a child's early home environment has upon his or her development?

Consider Proverbs 22:6 when presenting your response.

3. What influence do you feel your environment as a child has had upon the place which you have now achieved in your personal growth and development?

4. Some have said that personality is formed by two, or six, or twelve years of age. Others say personality is continuously re-formed throughout life. State your belief in this matter.

5. As an adult, should you be concerned about the type of people with whom you keep company? Explain. Cite the difference Christ made between who he chose as his close friends and those he treated as his acquaintances.

6. What words of wisdom do you have for the Christian who finds himself trapped in a seemingly unbearable living environment?

7. Comment on the statement, 'You shouldn't expect your ship to come in unless you have sent one out.' Relate this to Joseph's situation in Genesis 39:20-23.

8. What are some specific things you might do to create an environment for growth in your life?

ATTITUDE FOR GROWTH

1. King Solomon wrote, 'For as he thinketh in his heart, so is he.' (Proverbs 23:7 - KJV)

A. What significance do you think this has upon a person's inner happiness?

B. Could this have any implications which influence the effectiveness of a person's ability to help others?

2. In your own words, define the terms 'pessimistic' and 'optimistic'.

A. In what way can these attitudes affect the life of the average believer?

B. In what ways have they influenced your life?

3. Make a list of your five closest friends. On a scale from one to ten, ten representing a positive attitude and one representing a negative attitude, rate the attitude of each one.

A. Did you find a general pattern among your friends? Explain.

B. Read Proverbs 13:20. What possible influence could your friends have upon your attitude?

4. Write a one-line sentence which sums up your general attitude toward life.

A. Was this difficult to do? Why or why not?

B. What did you learn from this experience?

C.   Are there scriptures which you can cite which support your statement about your attitude? If so, what are they? If not, what changes need to be made in your sentence in order to make it compatible with Biblical teachings?

5. Read Luke 1:37, Romans 8:28 and Philippians 4:13. List an additional ten promises which God has given to man which should affect your attitude toward life.

6. Reflect upon the statement, 'There is more to life than happiness.' In what sense is this true? What influence should the vibrant Christian let this comment have upon his or her life?

7. Do you consider yourself to be an 'underachiever' or an 'overachiever'? Give evidence to support your answer. In what way does your attitude influence what kind of achiever you are?

8. Have you ever been motivated by the 'fear of failure'? Discuss yourself in this regard.

9. Comment on the question, 'If we live for tomorrow, will tomorrow ever come?' How does this relate to your attitude toward life?

10. For one twelve-hour period, carry a pencil and paper with you. List the number of times you make negative comments and the number of times you make positive comments.

A. How many positive and how may negative statements did you make? What was the ratio of positive to negative?

B. What does this reveal about your attitude?

C. Is your attitude as God-honoring as you would like for it to be? Explain. If it is not, what changes do you propose? If so, what suggestions do you have for people who are not satisfied with the nature of their attitude?

11. Read I Kings 15:25,26 and 16:25,26.

A. How did the influence of Omri and Nadab affect their people?

B. What principles can you draw from this which apply to the significance of your attitude to others in your ministry and home?

FLEXIBILITY FOR GROWTH

1. In general, do you consider yourself to be a flexible person? Explain, providing personal examples to support your response.

2. Do you believe that it is important to be flexible? If so, to what degree? If not, why not?

3. What factors do you think are most important when determining how flexible to be when working with others?

4. Develop your own definition for the word *dogmatism*.

   A.   Can dogmatism be a healthy part of your life? Explain.

   B.   Can dogmatism be harmful? Explain.

5. When can change be harmful to a person?

6. Explain your reaction to the statement, 'Change for the sake of change can be good.'

7. Are habits harmful or helpful? Explain. List at least five of your habits. Examine each one. Are they harmful or helpful? Briefly explain your reasoning.

8. Is change generally easy or difficult for you? Explain.

9. Interpret the meaning behind the prayer, 'Teach me to cry neither for the moon nor over spilt milk.' Share at least two illustrations from your life to either support or refute your interpretation.

VISION FOR GROWTH

1. Do you believe that vision is necessary for an *effective* life and ministry? Explain.

2. List at least five areas of your life in which vision could be helpful.

3. Why do some people fear failure?

   A.   Can this influence their visionary skill? Why or why not?

   B.   Has it ever affected your vision of the future? Explain.

4. Write a list entitled 'Before I die, I want to ...' Include at least 25 things which you would like to do before you die.

5. A.   Using the following format as your guide write your obituary as it would appear if you were to die today. Based upon your review of its contents, if you were to die today, would you have any regrets?

Mr./Ms._____died yesterday from _____.
He/She was a member of _____ and is survived by _____.
At the time of death he/she was working on becoming:
_____,

He/she will be remembered for: _____
_____

He/she will be mourned by: _____
_____
because _____
The world will suffer the loss of his/her contributions in the areas of: _____

He/she always wanted, but never got to:_____

_____

    B.   Using this same format indicate how you would ideally like your obituary to read when you die.

    C.   What changes did you make between the obituaries in A and B? Why did you make these changes?

    D.   Write between 100 and 500 words describing what you must do in order to make these changes become a reality.

7. How does Ephesians 5:15,16 relate to the concept of being visionary?

8. Can a vision for the future help you during difficult times? Explain.

9. Picture yourself in the ideal setting on earth. Now look around you. What do you see?

    A.   What time period are you living in?

    B.   Where did you choose to live?

    C.   With whom did you choose to live?

    D.   How old did you choose to be?

    E.   Are your values any different? Explain.

F. In what way has your family life been altered?

G. Describe your occupation.

H. What material goods do you possess?

I. Have your convictions altered? Explain.

J. Describe the kind of personality you elected to have.

Write at least three observations about the discrepancies and/or consistencies between your ideal world and the world in which you actually live. What possible implications could these have upon your vision of the future?

10. Set some personal goals for becoming the person you believe God would have you become by writing a paragraph response to each of the following statements:

A. To be a better person I will:

B. To be a better partner I will:

C. To be a better parent I will:

D. To be a better employee I will:

F. To be a better planner I will:

11. Was Paul a man of vision?

A. How was this evidenced?

B. Who are some of the other men of the faith who have demonstrated vision? Provide scriptural references to support your answer.

12. What three factors did Paul possess which are essential for a dream to become a reality?

13. Are there dangers to be aware of when it comes to 'dreaming dreams'? Explain.

14. Imagine the person who you would like to be ten years from now.

A. Write a description of that person in each aspect of his life. Include the following divisions: spiritual, ministry, family, mental, material, social, and physical.

B. Designate a piece of paper for each division and place its name at the top. After careful contemplation, write a list of the qualities you would like to have in each area ten years from now.

C. Take some time to review, analyze, and update this list. Write a general description of the person it describes. State internal characteristics as well as external. Do you feel that you can realistically become this person? Explain.

DIRECTION FOR GROWTH

General Background

1. What two things should a goal be able to be measured by?

2. What role should the Holy Spirit play in establishing and altering goals? What influence do James 4:15 and Acts 16:7 have on your answer?

3. Why are discipline, hard work, and faith important in goal accomplishment?

4. How can a Major Yearly Theme be helpful in establishing yearly goals?

5. Explain the terms microview, macroview, and suboptimum as they pertain to this chapter. Could they be of help to you as you establish your goals and objectives? Explain your answer.

6. Why is it important to be committed to each of your personal goals?

Creating a 'Personal Growth Profile'

1. Make copies of the General Worksheet (Exhibit 1).

    A. Using these forms, construct a general purpose statement for each major area of your life. Include each of the following:

Spiritual   Family
Physical   Mental
Ministry   Social
Material

B.   Write appropriate five- and one-year goals for
       each division.

2. Make copies of the Goal Sheet (Exhibit 2). Write your
   one-year goals for each division.

A.   Establish both immediate and future steps which
       need to be taken before each goal can be
       accomplished. Be sure to write the day each one
       will either be initiated or accomplished.

B.   Specify the minimum acceptable accomplishment
       and the maximum expected accomplishment for
       each goal.

3. Do you think that this total package of goals is
   accomplishable in the time you have specified? If not,
   make the changes necessary so that you feel that they
   are realistic.

4. Write an overall theme for the year.

5. Do each of your goals seem to support the yearly theme?

6. Put the General Worksheets and Goal Sheets into a
   loose leaf notebook to create your own Personal
   Growth Profile. Use index dividers to separate each of

the major divisions. Make a title sheet for the notebook and a 'table of contents' so that goals can be referred to easily during the year.

A Review of the Completed Personal Growth Profile

1. Do you feel hesitant about letting other people see the goals which you have established for yourself? Why do you think that this is or is not so? Do you think your feelings are healthy?

2. Are you looking forward to carrying out the daily process of seeing these goals become a reality? Explain your reasoning.

3. What did you learn about goals as a result of carrying out this exercise?

4. Was it easy or difficult to write yearly goals? Explain.

5. Did you consult with your spouse or other people in creating this notebook? If so, were their suggestions and insights helpful? What problems arose or could have arisen as a result of the counsel of others? If not, why not? What problems arose or could have arisen as a result of avoiding the counsel of others?

6. Write a paper (500 words or more) in which you describe your feeling toward the concept of goals. Be sure to use scripture to support *each* point.

7. Read the following scriptures. Write a paragraph for each one, indicating how it could or should influence a Christian's attitude toward goals.

Proverbs 16:9

Matthew 25:31-46

John 14:21

John 15:12

Acts 9:1-19

Acts 16:6,7

Romans 8:5,6,14-16

I Corinthians 9:24-26

I Corinthians 14:40

II Corinthians 5:6-10

II Corinthians 9:6-8

Philippians 3:13-14

Philippians 4:4-7

James 2:17

James 4:13-17

II Peter 3:18

GENERAL WORKSHEET   *Exhibit 1*

Area of Life:_____

General Purpose Statement:_____

Yearly Theme:_____

Long Range Goals:

    1._____

     _____

    2._____

     _____

    3._____

     _____

    4._____

     _____

One Year Goals:

    1._____

     _____

    2._____

     _____

    3._____

     _____

    4._____

     _____

GOAL SHEET

Exhibit 2

Goal: *What is to be accomplished?*

_____

_____

_____

Goal Verse _____

Date to begin __/__/__ Date to be accomplished __/__/__

Financial Commitment $ _____ Time Commitment _____

Steps to be taken towards the accomplishment of this goal:

Immediate Steps   *Date to be initiated or accomplished*

1.   __/__/__

2.   __/__/__

3.   __/__/__

Future Steps

1.   __/__/__

2.   __/__/__

3.   __/__/__

Maximum Expected Accomplishment_____

_____

Minimum Expected Accomplishment_____

_____